The Sovereign State
of Boogedy Boogedy
and Other Plays

The Sovereign State of Boogedy Boogedy
and Other Plays

by

Lonnie Carter

LOCUST HILL PRESS
West Cornwall, CT
1986

Iz She Izzy . . . reprinted by permission from *Scripts*, vol. 1, no. 7 (April-May 1972), pp. 45–71.

Waiting for G reprinted by permission from *Yale/Theatre*, vol. 5, special issue (Winter 1974).

The Sovereign State of Boogedy Boogedy reprinted by permission from *Yale/Theatre*, vol. 7, no. 3 (Spring 1976).

Library of Congress Cataloging-in-Publication Data

Carter, Lonnie, 1942–
  The sovereign state of Boogedy Boogedy and other plays.

  I. Title.
PS3553.A782S6   1986   812'.54   86-18503
ISBN 0-933951-04-3 (pbk.)

Cover design by Adriane Stark

Manufactured in the United States of America

For my family

and for Howard Stein

with special thanks to Julia Devlin,
Robert Brustein, Leo Jones
and Arnold Weinstein

Contents

Introduction

We live swimming in a sea of words. Talking, reading, hearing, teaching, signalling, hinting. Since human beings first stood up on two feet and discovered the power of speech, words have become more and more an irrevocable part of our being. If language were taken away from the human race tomorrow, our civilization would cease functioning: Charlie Chaplin and Buster Keaton being dead, there's virtually no one alive who could function without words, spoken or written or computerized.

Yet—this is the worst part—we know that our words would betray us. "Betray" in both senses, conveying what we don't mean and revealing what we would rather conceal. The first word was, if not the first lie, surely at least the first misstatement, and matters have only gotten worse as our dependence on words has increased. Wittgenstein's views of the imprecision of language have set the final seal on the matter, though we didn't need him to tell us to distrust what people say, which is folk wisdom in every culture and every language. "I am a Corinthian. All Corinthians are liars." The paradox of languages starts early and stays permanent, not so much an unwanted house guest as a frightening but necessary servant. Or as T.S. Eliot said, or rather had Sweeney say, "But I gotta use words when I talk to you." Or as Gertrude Stein said, or to be more precise as she had Virgil Thomson have Susan B. Anthony sing, "Do you know because I tell you so, or do you know, do you Know?"

A thing which is both vitally necessary and impossible to use is an inevitable source of comedy or tragedy. The

oracle said Oedipus would kill his father and marry his
mother. So he left home, killed an old man in a fit of temper
on the road, and married an older woman who, at least in the
Sophocles version, told him not to be silly, dear, all men
dream of sleeping with their mothers. At the other extreme
is the wife in the Ogden Nash poem who, when her husband
scoffed at her gourmet cuisine, looked in her cookbook for
one last recipe and saw "Croques Monsieur," which she did,
dining alone every night thereafter in Brillat-Savarin splen-
dor.

And midway between Sophocles and Ogden Nash, or
perhaps combining them, are the plays of Lonnie Carter,
whom it has taken me far too many words to lead up to.
Every playwright loves words with a bitter passion—when
people called Bernard Shaw's plays wordy, he used to ask
them if they'd call a painting too painty—but Lonnie's affair
with them is like no other in its gleeful and terrifying com-
pleteness. Other writers build edifices of words; the essence
of the building is in the structure, not the bricks. Lonnie
builds mad whirligigs with them, the verbal equivalents of
Gaudi, or Simon Rodilla's Watts Towers. Piles of words to
toboggan down, lumps of words to throw at people, caves of
words to nestle in, basketsful of loose words to scatter
before astonished, amazed, amused, haunted, daunted au-
diences.

We've been friends for twenty years now: Lonnie was
the first person I met the first day I arrived at the Yale
School of Drama, where we were both about to be playwrit-
ing students. (He stayed; I branched out). In our very first
conversation, that first evening, we talked about words. I
still remember that he told me about a play of his in which a
tired old man said, "I have had done." A few years later I
directed a reading of a play of his, and learned something
about his methods (and about tactics every writer uses to
some extent) when a patient in a doctor's examining room
asked if he could put his shirt back on and the nurse replied,
"Why, you clod? Are you cold?" I got him to admit that "you
clod" was a slip of the typewriter he had retained for fun,
and made him cut it, because the nurse had no intense
dramatic reason for calling the patient a clod, but I always
missed the line afterwards, and have felt guilty about delet-

ing it ever since. Accidents like that are the inner mind's moments of glory, and should be treasured. And the patient, who was the play's ineffectual hero, *was* a clod.

After leaving Yale I made my New York directing debut with two one-acts of Lonnie's, crammed into the back room of a bar in the then-dangerous and unfashionable East Village called the Old Reliable Theatre Tavern. One of them was about a physicist (played with memorable Chekhovian wistfulness by the late Neil Flanagan) who had discovered a way to create either timeless time or spaceless space; I forget which. I remember his mercenary nephew, a manufacturer who spoke of "the place where I manufacture which means make with my hands which I don't but you know what I mean." That unnerving string of contradictions and half-turns has always summed up for me the particular nature of Lonnie's brilliance, which is to hew strictly as a writer to the literal meaning of every word, while simultaneously conceding that it has nothing at all to do with the way the word is used. As Lewis Carroll's White Knight said to Alice, that's not the name of the song, that's what the name of the song is called.

The disparity is, at varying times in Lonnie's work, tragic and funny and giddy and exhausting—I won't deny that I often get exhausted by it—and sweet and shrill and harrowing. All the language games in Lonnie would not be of much use if there were not passion and a visionary imagination behind them, and he has both. The shortest piece in the volume my verbosity is currently preventing you from reading was written for a revue staged at the Yale Rep, at the height of the Watergate revelations. The resplendent Alvin Epstein, who had created the role of Lucky in the original Broadway production of *Waiting for Godot*, was a vital part of the Rep's company then, as actor and director, and his presence inspired Lonnie to one of the most nightmarish visions he has ever written down, in which Nixon became Beckett's Lucky, a gaunt, driven stream of words on the end of a rope pulled not by Pozzo but by Nixon's rich pal Rebozo. Though not far from Beckett's method, inherited for this particular occasion from his former employer Joyce, the words of Nixon-Lickie are very far from Lucky's broken fragments of teleological pondering; they roar in the stream of unmitigated hate, bigotry, spite, and suspicion that was revealed in a more leisurely fashion by the White House transcripts. In Lonnie's version, it became one of the most racking events I ever witnessed onstage—the accumulated malignity of Tricky Dick set out stroke by stroke, as if by a great satirical cartoonist.

I speak of the Lickie speech because it is the smallest and most maneuverable of the whirligigs in this volume, and because its historical position as an occasional piece calls for the explanation. For the rest, I don't propose to go into details: A prefator should know his boundaries, and it's no business of mine to tell readers what to think of Lonnie Carter's plays, what they are and how they work. Anyway, to do so would spoil for you the fun I have had reading them, hearing them read, seeing them performed on the rare occasions when actors, directors, and producers with quick enough brains can be found to take a risk on them. It is absolutely outside my purview to explain who Ruby Begonia is, what is funny about basting a decoy, or how "As the bishop said to the actress" came into common usage.

I will only say that a magic, if somewhat menacing, castle can be built of words by anyone who loves them enough (or perhaps, by anyone who loves them too much), and that a magic castle, even if menacing, is a refreshing place to be for a while, and a very good place to learn that things are not what we say they are, they are what they are and then there is what we say. If you could read my mind, you would understand precisely what I mean. Since this is not humanly possible, let me present Lonnie Carter's words: You can read them and understand precisely what they say, because they are just words, and therefore do not, in the larger sense, mean anything. Though of course in writing they mean, and in fact are, everything.

Michael Feingold, 1986
Theater Critic, *The Village Voice*

A Director's Note
on the Title Play

Lonnie Carter is one of the best-known and least-produced American playwrights. Upon reading his plays, many people remark: "I can't decide if he is a madman or a genius." Like many artists, he is a bit of both; and like many playwrights, including Shakespeare, his work does not come alive until it is spoken aloud.

Carter's works are sometimes criticized because he seems to be writing about many things at once. He is. In many ways, his love of language (and languages) frequently leads to a wealth of ideas and imagery that produces both a challenge and a vitality that is truly unique.

When meeting the challenge of *The Sovereign State of Boogedy Boogedy*, it might be helpful to use "The serious side of nonsense" as a working title. The humorous aspects of the script are often immediately apparent, but a successful production also requires attention to Carter's issues of concern. Some of these issues are the preoccupation and interpretation of dreams, the irreparable damage of warfare, the corruption of political and corporate powers, and the presentation of a world in which one should be held accountable for one's actions.

While many issues are represented in Carter's script, the play, by and large, is presentational in nature. Ultimately, the actors' recognition of the audience is perhaps even more natural than the tendency to "pretend they are not there," which so frequently occurs in the presentation of realistic dramas.

The Sovereign State of Boogedy Boogedy is a three-act play that seems to have three different styles of presentation. In Act

One, the mode is set by Abed-nego; Act Two is led by the antics of Shadrach; and in Act Three, Meshach switches the focus from the trial of Nebuchadnezzar to the trial of Daniel/Danielle—the holy man who allowed innocent people to be devoured in the lion's den. The persona of each of the characters guides one of the three acts; the collective persona of the trio leads the play.

The relationship between Nebuchadnezzar and Danielle is a symbiotic one. He is the dreamer; she is the dreamless interpreter. Together their efforts provide a completion to the visions, and we are presented with one visionary. This interdependence is also apparent during the business of the Court.

The pursuit of justice is evident in all of Carter's work, but perhaps most clear in *The Sovereign State of Boogedy Boogedy*. Even though God has already decided the outcome of this trial, Judges Shadrach, Meshach, and Abed-nego, driven in their dialogue by the energy of thought, must put King Nebuchadnezzar on trial for his crimes much as Sisyphus must push the rock back up the hill.

Dennis Zacek, 1986
Artistic Director, Victory Gardens

Iz She Izzy
Or Iz He Ain'tzy
Or Iz They Both

MUSIC BY ROBERT MONTGOMERY

for Richard Gilman

FIRST PERFORMANCE:

March 1970, Yale Repertory Theatre, New Haven, Connecticut

Joan Pape as the Court Recorder
David Ackroyd as Justice "Choo-Choo" Justice
Steven Van Benschoten as A. T. "Ernie" Law
Elizabeth Parrish as Suzy Quzer
Louis Plante as Tallahassee Yo-yo
David Ackroyd as Isabella Borgward
James Brick as Ferdinand "Bongo" Kknot

Directed by Richard Gilman

THE PLAYERS:

COURT RECORDER
JUSTICE "CHOO-CHOO" JUSTICE
A. T. "ERNIE" LAW
SUZY QUZER
TALLAHASSEE YO-YO
ISABELLA BORGWARD
FERDINAND "BONGO" KKNOT

THE SCENE:

A Court of Law. ISABELLA BORGWARD's office.

David Ackroyd as Justice "Choo-Choo" Justice
(*Photograph by Constance Brewster*)

A court of law. A. T. "ERNIE" LAW, SUZY QUZER, TALLAHASSEE YO-YO, *and the* COURT RECORDER.

COURT RECORDER: All rise for Justice Justice.

JUSTICE "CHOO-CHOO" JUSTICE, *singing "Chattanooga Choo-Choo," pedals in on a toy train.*

Justice Justice! This is no way to begin a trial.

CHOO-CHOO: Call me Choo-Choo. (*He dances with the* COURT RECORDER.)
Pardon me, boys
Is that the Chattanooga Choo-Choo
Woo Woo . . .
What's the matter, don't you like that number? How about "The Wabash Blues"? I'll do any number but "The Acheson, Topeka, and the Santa Barbara."

COURT RECORDER: Santa Fe.

CHOO-CHOO: That's why I won't do it. This is no kangaroo court, it's a court full of kangaroos . . .

A. T. "ERNIE" LAW *and* TALLAHASSEE YO-YO *make authentic kangaroo sounds.*

Where's the jury?

COURT RECORDER: Hung on another case.

CHOO-CHOO: Drunk again, huh? Let them finish that case, but as soon as they sober up, get them in here. All right, who are you people?

LAW: A. T. "Ernie" Law.

CHOO-CHOO: I know you. You defended Jud Mudd, the man who put air pollution into summer camps.

SUZY QUZER: Suzy Quzer. I'm innocent.

CHOO-CHOO: Just minding your p's and, huh, Suzy?

TALLAHASSEE YO-YO: Tal Yo-yo.

CHOO-CHOO: Tal Yo-yo? (*To the tune of "Tell Laura I Love Her."*) "Tal Yo-yo I love her!"

COURT RECORDER: Justice Justice wants your full name.

TAL YO-YO:
> Tallahassee Yo-yo
> The finest Yo-yo made

CHOO-CHOO (*pulling out his own yo-yo and playing with it*): Oh yeah, what about this one?

TAL YO-YO: I'm Suzy's mouthpiece.

CHOO-CHOO: In the fight game, huh, Suzy? Your weight welter? Say, didn't I see you on a card up in Bangor?

COURT RECORDER: Justice Justice, it's time for swearing in.

CHOO-CHOO: Swearing in?

COURT RECORDER: Swearing in!

CHOO-CHOO: Who are you?

COURT RECORDER: The Court Recorder.

CHOO-CHOO: Well, press your fast backwards. You swear in this court, I'll hold you in contempt and hate you forever.

LAW: Let's get on with this trial. You're standing in the way of Justice.

CHOO-CHOO (*getting out of his own way*): I beg your pardon.

LAW: Miss Quzer, take the stand.

CHOO-CHOO: You won't get far with that stand, Suzy. We'll have you picked up before you pick it up, if not before before.

LAW: Any further delay will mean getting nothing done before recess.

CHOO-CHOO:
> Yea recess
> One one thousand
> Two one thousand
> Three one thousand
> Four
> Five one thousand
> Six one thousand
> Seven one thousand
> Eight

LAW: Your Honor!

CHOO-CHOO: I see Ernie Law standing by the witness bench.

LAW: This is a murder case!

CHOO-CHOO: That bad, huh? All right. Oli Oli in free! All right, let's begin. Who's charged with what, what charges are on which and who's on second?

LAW: Suzy Quzer is charged with the murder of Isabella Borgward.

CHOO-CHOO: Infamous Isabella?

LAW: None other.

CHOO-CHOO: Madame of a journalistic house of ill repute?

LAW: You're the Justice, don't you know what case this is?

CHOO-CHOO (*holding up his briefcase*): Not the one the jury's hung on, that's for sure.

LAW: I have a writ of *habeas corpus*.

CHOO-CHOO: What's the matter, can't you speak English? *Habeas corpus* what?

LAW: Writ.

CHOO-CHOO: Wrong.

SUZY: Do I swear to tell the whole truth and nothing but the truth so help me? So help me?

CHOO-CHOO: You do. Let's hurry it up, where's the evidence?

LAW: What evidence?

CHOO-CHOO: Exactly. What evidence?

LAW: Where's what evidence?

CHOO-CHOO: No evidence, huh? Just as I thought.

LAW: Justice Justice, will you please let me take the first step?

CHOO-CHOO: Say "Choo-Choo, may I?"!

LAW: Choo-Choo, may I?

CHOO-CHOO: You may take one baby and three giants, but don't step on any cracks or I'll cut you up with my scissors step.

LAW: Now Miss Quzer, tell the court your precise reactions when you found the body of Isabella Borgward.

SUZY: "Izzy, Izzy, is that you?" I said.

LAW: Izzy?

SUZY: "Is that you?" I said.

LAW: You called Isabella Borgward "Izzy"?

TAL YO-YO: I object.

SUZY: She didn't.

CHOO-CHOO: Overruled, Yo-yo.

SUZY: She did.

CHOO-CHOO: Sustained.

LAW: What was the objection?

CHOO-CHOO: Overruled and sustained.

LAW: You can't do both.

CHOO-CHOO: Then I won't do either.

LAW: You can't do neither.

CHOO-CHOO: Then I won't do neither nor both and if that's not enough I won't do all three.

LAW: Miss Quzer, what else did you say?

SUZY: "It must be me," said I. "It must be me."

LAW: Did you think *you* were dead?

SUZY: Why not?

LAW: Or, Miss Quzer, were you *hoping* you were dead, realizing that you had murdered Isabella Borgward?

TAL YO-YO: I object.

SUZY (*breaking down*): Yes, I did it. I did it!

LAW: How did it start, Suzy?

SUZY: It all started in Izzy's office.

ISABELLA BORGWARD's office. ISABELLA is clearly played by the actor playing CHOO-CHOO.

ISABELLA (*on the phone*): Hello, Bingo? No? Bingo's calling numbers? OK. Give me Bongo . . . Bongo's playing Bingo? How many cards does he have? G-46 and he's got three ways. I hope Bongo doesn't get beat. My best of Bingo to Bongo. Tell him I got two cards for the next game. Let me have Bango . . . Bango's what? . . . Started a rival game of Bango rivaling neighborhood Bingo? No. Call the Bungo squad. I suppose Bengo's not available. . . . Oh, he is. Well, you tell Bengo to call Bungo, hit Bango, cheer Bongo and pay Bingo. Get my lingo? By the way, Jingo, how come you're free to answer the phone? . . . Oh, that's how you play dingaling. (*She hangs up.*)
    I'm Isabella Borgward
    Editor-publisher of *Skin*
    The magazine that's beauty-deep
    I'm Isabella Borgward
    Boss of Gloss
(*Singing*).
    Skin's real
    Feel
    Pages of *Skin*
    Are pages of skin
    Torn from actual flesh
    Born of supple nitties
    Enormous gritties
    We're bumpy
    We're grindy
    Come lose
    Your mindy

    Don't peep
    Skin-dive

    Skin
    Is so into
    Skin
    It's bone

So buy *Skin*
Love *Skin*
Adore *Skin*

'Cause it's by skin
Of skin
And for skin

I'm Isabella Borgward

And somebody's out to kill me.

SUZY QUZER (*entering, singing*):
I've been sailing along
This moonlit day
On the sauce I'm ever after
This moonlit day

ISABELLA: Suzy, you've got to help me.

SUZY: Izzy, Izzy, ask me for help. Ask me, ask me, Izzy. I'll help for the asking, Izzy. Help help. Ask, Izzy, ask.

ISABELLA: I beg your pardon.

SUZY: Izzy, Izzy, ask me for help. Ask me, Izzy, ask me.

ISABELLA: Help!

SUZY: What is it, Izzy?

ISABELLA: Will you stop calling me "Izzy"?

SUZY: That's the help you ask for? Not calling you "Izzy" is a help?

ISABELLA: Suzy.

SUZY: Don't call me "Suzy."

ISABELLA: What am I supposed to call you?

SUZY: What am I supposed to call you?

ISABELLA: I asked you first.

SUZY: Don't call me.

ISABELLA: I'll call you.

SUZY: Call me and I'll call you.

ISABELLA: Help!

SUZY: Ask me, Izzy, ask me.

ISABELLA: I need a boost.

SUZY: Give me your left foot.

ISABELLA: Which one?

SUZY: Didn't you hear me? I said "Give me your left foot."

ISABELLA: Which one?

SUZY: Two left feet, huh? Well, give me your right foot.

ISABELLA: Make up your mind, here's my left foot.

SUZY: That's your right foot.

ISABELLA: What's wrong with that?

SUZY: Afraid I won't hold you up?

ISABELLA: You're no bandit.

SUZY: Stick up both your feet and reach for the sky.

ISABELLA: I will not. I'm taking a long walk off a short pier.

SUZY: Can I come along?

ISABELLA: Lead the way.

SUZY: What about the boost?

ISABELLA: Help!

SUZY: Help has arrived.

ISABELLA: Somebody's out to kill me.

> *TAL YO-YO enters as a Western Union messenger.*

SUZY: Who?

ISABELLA: Who are you?

TAL YO-YO: Tallahassee Yo-yo, the finest Yo-yo made. Want to see my locket?

ISABELLA: Your sweetheart?

SUZY: Your mother?

ISABELLA: Your yo-yo?

TAL YO-YO: My multicolored Kaiser-Fraser hot rod.

ISABELLA: Want to dash that jalopy for cash?

TAL YO-YO: What kind of wheels you got?

ISABELLA: A Stutz Polecat.

TAL YO-YO: How are your cams?

ISABELLA: Bushed.

TAL YO-YO: Your regulator?

ISABELLA: I go twice a day.

TAL YO-YO: Automatic?

ISABELLA: Like clockwork.

TAL YO-YO: Come out to the strip.

ISABELLA: What kind of clothes shouldn't I wear?

TAL YO-YO: The drag strip.

ISABELLA: Oh, I'll wear my blue taffeta.

TAL YO-YO: But be ready for action. This is how I do it. At the line, I drop my Kaiser-Fraser in L for Lunge and stomp on it. When I hit around a hundred, I throw it R for Race till I hit 250.

ISABELLA: 250!

TAL YO-YO: It's got a thousand horses.

ISABELLA: That's funny. That hood doesn't look big enough to hold a small pony.

SUZY: Say, Yo-yo, you don't look so tough to me.

TAL YO-YO: I'm very gentle. I think of myself as a gentle greaser.

SUZY: What's this on the flip side of your locket?

TAL YO-YO: That's my secret compartment.

SUZY: And in that secret compartment?

ISABELLA: A gun! You're out to gun me down!

TAL YO-YO: I gun my Kaiser-Fraser, lady.

ISABELLA: You gun your Kaiser-Fraser lady and now you want to gun me. Out, out, damned lout! (*She runs him out.*)

TAL YO-YO: I have a message.

ISABELLA: Try Western Union.

TAL YO-YO (*coming back in*): I am Western Union.

ISABELLA: Oh, you are Western Union. Why didn't you say so in the first place?

TAL YO-YO: In the first place I thought you'd know from my uniform.

ISABELLA: Listen here, boy, in the first place, when a man dresses like a woman, where's the first place it hangs out?

TAL YO-YO: The front? A bar? The front of a bar?

ISABELLA: That's the first place.

TAL YO-YO: But I'm not dressed like a woman.

ISABELLA: Then, how would I know you in the first place?

TAL YO-YO: You're right. Would you know me in the second place?

ISABELLA: If you hung out in the back.

TAL YO-YO: Sign here.

ISABELLA: Front or back?

TAL YO-YO: Doesn't matter.

ISABELLA: Does to me, Billie.

TAL YO-YO: Call me Tallahassee.

ISABELLA: Why did you come here now?

TAL YO-YO: Call me Tallahassee.

ISABELLA: This wind tunnel's got an echo in it. Tell me, Tallahassee, why do I call you Tallahassee?

TAL YO-YO: I'm from Tallahassee.

ISABELLA: Glad I asked. Why Yo-yo?

TAL YO-YO: I'll give you three guesses.

ISABELLA: Something for nothing. 'Cause you go down?

TAL YO-YO: No. Guess again.

ISABELLA: 'Cause you go up?

TAL YO-YO: No. Last guess.

ISABELLA: 'Cause you go up *and* down?

TAL YO-YO: No. Actually, Yo-yoville is a suburb of Tallahassee. I was born up in Yo-yoville, then my parents moved down to Tallahassee, then I moved back up to Yo-yoville.

ISABELLA: Certainly are a mysterious fellow.

TAL YO-YO: I almost forgot—
     Happy deathday to you
     Happy deathday to you
     Happy deathday, Isabella
     Happy deathday to you

ISABELLA: What a surprise! I'm so thrilled! I didn't think anyone would remember! But my deathday was last week.

TAL YO-YO: It's belated.

ISABELLA: So it is. And it's signed.

SUZY: So it is.

ISABELLA: It's time for my phone call.

The phone rings. SUZY *answers.*

SUZY: Hello? Who's calling? Wrong number. (*She hangs up.*) It was for you.

ISABELLA: Just as I thought. Why did you hang up?

SUZY: Wrong number.

The phone rings. TAL YO-YO *answers.*

TAL YO-YO: Hello? Who's calling? Wrong number. (*He hangs up.*) It was for you.

ISABELLA: Just as I thought. Why did you hang up?

TAL YO-YO: Wrong number.

The phone rings. ISABELLA *answers.*

ISABELLA: Hello? Who's calling? Wrong number. (*She hangs up.*) It was for you.

TAL YO-YO *and* SUZY: Me!

ISABELLA: I mean me. Just as I thought. Why did I hang up?

TAL YO-YO *and* SUZY: Wrong number.

ISABELLA: Right. My number's not up yet.

The phone rings. ISABELLA *answers.*

Hello? (*She pulls out two bingo cards.*) O-63, G-45, N-free, I-21, B-3, BINGO! Put on Bongo. I beat you, Bongo. What do you mean I didn't win fair? This is a fine kettle of drum. Don't percuss me out, I'll skin your skins, I'll drum your sticks, you chicken. (*She hangs up.*)

The phone rings three times. No one moves.

Can you beat that?

The phone rings four times. No one moves.

TAL YO-YO: Miss Isabella?

ISABELLA: Shhh.

The phone rings once. No one moves.

SUZY: Izzy?

ISABELLA: Shhh!

The phone rings twice. No one moves.

That's him. Out.

TAL YO-YO *and* SUZY *leave.*

Hello? Yes, darling. Of course, *darling.*

The scene changes to the courtroom. CHOO-CHOO *absent.*

LAW: Get to the point, Miss Quzer. You've confessed to the murder of Isabella Borgward.

SUZY: I have not. I'm innocent.

LAW: Will the Court Recorder read back the transcript?

COURT RECORDER: All right. (*Breaking down.*) "I did it. I did it."

SUZY: I take it all back.

TAL YO-YO: I object.

LAW: Your Honor. Your Honor? Where is Justice Justice?

CHOO-CHOO (*pedaling in on his toy train*): Right here on the right track, Ernie, and don't you forget it and who I am, the well-known arbiter in the case of the State vs. Constantin Dipshit in which the historic decision that a man cannot be discriminated against for an off-color name was passed down and out.

SUZY: I'm innocent.

CHOO-CHOO: Stick to your guns, Suzy. Or whatever you used.

LAW: Your Honor, I object most strenuously.

CHOO-CHOO: Easy, A. T., you'll live longer.

LAW: Is that a threat?

CHOO-CHOO: A message from your Heart Association.

COURT RECORDER: Excuse me, Your Honor, but that comes later in the program.

CHOO-CHOO: Are we on TV?

COURT RECORDER: Closed-circuit cable pay.

CHOO-CHOO: I told you not to get us on either one of those hayburners. What kind of a bookie are you? One more blooper and I'll make you a bookend. Look at the odds on TV Program. 1–5000. Why that's outrageous. Just the other day that stumblebum bolted at the gate, fell on the first rail, impaled the jockey on the last pole, somersaulted over the line and *still* finished twelfth in a field of ten. Now what about Closed-Circuit Cable Pay? Ahh, now there's a filly who should've stayed in Camden. Well, it's only moola. I'll put a fin on the nose. Anybody else? Come on, hurry up. This is a court of law.

LAW: You'd never know it.

CHOO-CHOO: What did you say?

LAW: I said "You'd never know it."

CHOO-CHOO: You'd Never Know It. You'd Never Know It, huh? How much weight is he carrying? Will he run on grass or does he need something stronger?

LAW: Your Honor, if my sense of justice were not so acute . . .

CHOO-CHOO: I'll take a shower during recess.

LAW: If I did not so strongly desire to see the murderers punished, the murderers of a brave and noble lady . . .

CHOO-CHOO: Brave and noble? Infamous Isabella? Say, Law, just what was your connection with this brave and noble lady?

LAW: We met one spring in traffic court. She was accused of driving a multicolored Kaiser-Fraser under the influence.

CHOO-CHOO: Under the influence? Is that near the viaduct?

COURT RECORDER: Your Honor, do you want me to record this?

CHOO-CHOO: No, and tell those kangaroos to take a breather.

Loud breathing sounds from the kangaroo impersonators, A. T. LAW *and* TAL YO-YO.

Wise 'roos, huh? Tell them to go soak their heads in their pouches.

The COURT RECORDER *and* SUZY *make sounds of heads soaking in pouches contrapuntally with loud breathing.*

I'll speak to them. Herd on out.

LAW, YO-YO, *the* COURT RECORDER, *and* SUZY *all make sounds of herding on out.*

Guess I taught a 'roo or two a thing. Now where were we?

LAW: In traffic court.

CHOO-CHOO: Yes. Brave and noble. Under the influence. Driving a multicolored Kaiser-Fraser. You'd have to be brave and under the influence.

TAL YO-YO: I object.

CHOO-CHOO: Yo-yo, let me see your docket.

TAL YO-YO: May I approach the bench?

CHOO-CHOO: Just don't be sneaky about it. I said your docket, not your locket.

TAL YO-YO: My docket! It's gone.

CHOO-CHOO: Nobody leaves this room, till we find this man's docket. Now, what did it look like, Yo-yo?

TAL YO-YO: Just an ordinary docket.

CHOO-CHOO: Nothing unusual at all? No identifying marks?

TAL YO-YO: Why yes. There's a small scar above the left margin.

COURT RECORDER: Excuse me, Your Honor, but I suspect one of those kangaroos.

CHOO-CHOO: The strong silent one. Let's reconstruct the scene. The 'roos herd on out and the strong silent one steals away with the docket. It's perfect. Not a trace. Not a sound.

COURT RECORDER: But! Will the 'roo return to the scene of the mime?

TAL YO-YO: I object.

CHOO-CHOO: Easy, Yo-yo, your string's taut. That's the thing about string, teach it once and it stays taught. Oh, you don't like that, huh, Yo-yo, go up and down once more like a real yo-yo and we'll see whose loop-the-loop's around whose neck. Oh, you don't like that one either, huh, Yo-yo, walk the dog on my book and I'll throw the bench at you. And if you don't like that one either, you can walk your dog in the park on somebody else's book and let him throw the bench at you. I regret I have but one bench to throw, but for the money I paid to get this job, I'm lucky I got a pot to put peas in.

COURT RECORDER: Careful, Justice Justice, you were almost thrown off Closed-Circuit Cable Pay.

CHOO-CHOO: Am I the one riding that nag?

LAW: You admit the position you hold was bought? How can you, Justice Justice, how can you preside knowing a transgression of the law has brought you to this august court?

CHOO-CHOO: *De gustibus non gustibutandum cum gustibus est.*

LAW: According to tastes it is not to be tasted with tastes?

CHOO-CHOO: It means get it out of your mouth, Law. What do you say there, Suzy?

SUZY: What do you say there, Choo-Choo?

CHOO-CHOO: I say "What do you say there, Suzy?"

SUZY: If only we could forget about this and get away from it all.

CHOO-CHOO: That's a wonderful idea, Suzy. Let's go to a nice place by the sea and get scrod. Ever hear that word in the pluperfect passive before?

SUZY: I love seafood. The smell of fresh carp roasting on an open fire.

CHOO-CHOO: Hook, line, and stinker.

SUZY: I'm just a sucker for the great outdoors.

CHOO-CHOO: I think I'll pass that line by.

SUZY: Want to hear me call duck?

CHOO-CHOO: Wait till seven and the rates drop. Will that be collect or person-to-duck?

SUZY: What do you know about hunting? Freezing all day in a blind.

CHOO-CHOO: For frozen duck?

SUZY: The drinking it takes just to keep alive. At the end of the day I'm as blind as the decoy.

CHOO-CHOO: Duck is so greasy. What about decoy?

SUZY: Well, I cook decoy at 440 and baste a lot.

CHOO-CHOO: Well done. No, make that medium-rare.

LAW: What about Isabella Borgward?

CHOO-CHOO: Let's move it on out, Suzy, you and me, kid, we're going all the way. (*To the* COURT RECORDER.) Don't disturb my chambers and bring my pot with the peas in.

CHOO-CHOO and SUZY pedal out. The COURT RECORDER *follows.*

LAW: We met one spring in traffic court. She was accused of driving a multicolored Kaiser-Fraser under the influence.

TAL YO-YO: I object. That was my Kaiser-Fraser.

LAW: Why was she driving your Kaiser-Fraser?

TAL YO-YO: It was hers as soon as she got in. I loved her.

LAW: *I* loved her!

TAL YO-YO and LAW (*together*): Then you're "Darling"! No! I didn't make that call. Then who did? Bongo? No. Tell me about you and Isabella. You first.

LAW: You.

TAL YO-YO: I only saw her once before I delivered the deathday wish. She and Suzy Quzer came to see the multicolored Kaiser-Fraser.

The scene goes outside the courtroom to the Kaiser-Fraser hot rod. No properties. SUZY *watches as* ISABELLA *kicks the tires, slams the door, snaps the windshield wipers, pounds the fenders, yanks off the hood ornament, opens and slams the hood, washes the windows with her spit, adjusts the driver's seat,* SUZY'S *seat,* SUZY, *steering wheel,* SUZY'S *toy steering wheel, both seat belts, rolls all the windows down and up and down, fixes the rearview mirror, the rearview mirror's baby boots, sideview mirror,* SUZY, *FM tuner, bar, stereo,* SUZY'S *transistor, telephone,* SUZY'S *toy telephone, refrigerator, herself,* SUZY'S *self . . .*

ISABELLA: You drive.

SUZY takes driver's seat. ISABELLA SUZY'S. SUZY *adjusts the driver's seat,* ISABELLA'S *seat,* ISABELLA'S *physical seat, both seat belts, all mirrors, her transistor, her toy steering wheel, the rearview mirror's baby boots and dice, herself,* ISABELLA'S *self . . .*

SUZY: There's no key. Should we steal it anyway?

ISABELLA: Let's not.

They walk away.

Author's note: To facilitate what is very difficult pantomime indeed, the actors might recite the stage directions in the third person while performing the action. For example:

ISABELLA: ISABELLA *kicks the tires, slams the doors, etc., says,* "You drive."

Or better yet ISABELLA *might describe* SUZY's *actions, and vice versa.*

The scene goes back to LAW *and* TAL YO-YO *in the courtroom.*

LAW: She and Suzy stole cars!

TAL YO-YO: It was hers as soon as she got in. I loved her. Next time I left the key in.

Back to SUZY *and* ISABELLA *at the Kaiser-Fraser.*

SUZY: Izzy, the key's here.

ISABELLA: Just as I thought.

SUZY: Well, what are we waiting for? Izzy, are you scared?

ISABELLA: No, Suzy, I'm thinking. My life's an open book. My back has lost its binding. My pages have all been cut. I must save myself. I must. I've got to come out in paperback.

SUZY: Izzy, look in the back seat. A copy of your magazine *Skin.*

ISABELLA: A fan, Suzy. I have fans everywhere. Why? Because I give them what they want and need. What they love, Suzy. Smut.

SUZY: I love smut because it makes me feel all filled up and wholesome inside. It's enriched. Each word a picture. Each picture ten thousand words. Each ten thousand words in each and every word a message. A message of trust between you and lust.

ISABELLA: Easy, girl, you forget what we're here for.

SUZY: You're right. But what about the magazine?

ISABELLA: I got dibbies on seeing it first.

SUZY: I got dibbies on it!

ISABELLA: I called dibbies before you even saw it.

SUZY: You did not, I said "Look in the back seat, one of your magazines."

ISABELLA: And I called dibbies on it. I can't help it if you didn't hear my dibbies.

SUZY: Dibbies! I just called it.

The argument goes on. Back to LAW *and* TAL YO-YO *in the courtroom.*

LAW: Tell me, why did you love her?

TAL YO-YO: A certain something I can't explain, but the first time I saw her I called dibbies.

LAW: *I* called dibbies on her! What do you know about Isabella and me? Isabella and me!

The scene flashes back to ISABELLA *and* LAW.

Isabella, it's me, Ernie.

ISABELLA: Ernie Pyle?

LAW: No.

ISABELLA: Ernie Pyle of?

LAW: No.

ISABELLA: Am I close?

LAW: No.

ISABELLA: Tell me, don't be cruel.

LAW: You should know.

ISABELLA: You Should Know. You Should Know. How many hands does he stand? Say, did he sire You'd Never Know It?

LAW: No.

ISABELLA: Closed-Circuit Cable Pay?

LAW: Ernie Law!

ISABELLA: I know you, you defended Jud Mudd, the man who brought air pollution to Hialeah—I mean, summer camps.

LAW: Your lover!

ISABELLA: Horses do do dirty things, but you go too far.

LAW: Let me.

ISABELLA: Entertain me.

LAW: That comes with my going too far.

ISABELLA: Oh yeah?

LAW: Oh yeah.

ISABELLA: Oh yeah? I feel like an echo in a wind tunnel. I've already said that. I feel like a canyon in a wind tunnel whose echo hurts. Figure that one out and I'll give *you* dibbies.

LAW: Isabella, I love you.

ISABELLA: I'm promised to another.

LAW: I'll wait.

ISABELLA: Till he dies?

LAW: Till I kill him.

> *Frightened cries from* ISABELLA. *The scene flashes to* TAL YO-YO *and* LAW *in the courtroom.*

TAL YO-YO: So, you killed him.

LAW: Of course not. I didn't even know who he was. Is.

TAL YO-YO: Is he still alive or isn't he?

LAW: How should I know?

TAL YO-YO: But you *do* know Isabella is dead. *You* killed Isabella Borgward.

LAW: Preposterous. You did. Suzy did. You and "Darling" did. Then you killed "Darling."

TAL YO-YO: How do you know he's dead? For that matter how do you know he's a he?

LAW: What! You go on the stand right after recess and I'll expose your twisted heart.

TAL YO-YO: If only we had another judge. Can't we impeach him? My honor's at stake.

LAW: Her honor's at stake. The lunch recess is over. Where's His Honor?

The COURT RECORDER enters.

COURT RECORDER: His Honor's at steak.

CHOO-CHOO and SUZY pedal in.

CHOO-CHOO: More like hamburger. OK, Suzy Q, here we are, kid.

LAW: Your Honor, I call Tallahassee Yo-yo to the stand.

A new figure emerges to interrupt the proceedings.

NEW FIGURE: One second.

CHOO-CHOO: Who are you?

NEW FIGURE: Ferdinand Kknot.

CHOO-CHOO: K-n-o-t?

FERDINAND: K-*k*-n-o-t.

CHOO-CHOO: Any relation to Gary Ggnu?

FERDINAND: Three *g*'s?

CHOO-CHOO: I wouldn't put more than a fin on You'd Never Know It, but three *g*'s on Gary Ggnu?

FERDINAND: Gary goes!

CHOO-CHOO: Where? I mean, where do the three *g*'s go?

FERDINAND and CHOO-CHOO sing "Tri-Gam."

FERDINAND:

> One on Gary
> Two on Ggnu
> That's where the three *g*'s go

CHOO-CHOO:

> One on "golly"
> Two on "ggee"
> That's where the three *g*'s go

BOTH:
> One on "gamma"
> One on "gamma"
> One on "gamma"
> Gimme gimme gimme
> Some gamma gamma gamma
>
> That's where the Tri-Gam goes

CHOO-CHOO and FERDINAND give each other the Tri-Gam secret knee-knock.

FERDINAND: Ah, Choo-Choo, you're a sore for sightless eyes. What were some of our old routines? I've got one. Why don't we do the opening of Christopher Columbus?

CHOO-CHOO: Not that one, Bongo. I said not that one, Bongo. After all this is a Court of Law. We've got serious business. Definitely not that one, Bongo. This is an important trial. In the balance hangs a life.

SUZY: Help, help!

LAW: Just what is this Christopher Columbus routine?

CHOO-CHOO: You wouldn't like it at all. This guy named Columbus is discovered in Ohio stealing a mysterious uncharted map from a shady goon named Americus Suspicious, who got his info turning over a new leaf with his son Eric. Well, Columbus, map in hand, takes a plane in the rain for the mainland of Spain to see his old friend Trini Magellan, the pop singer, who has just hit the charts with "That Old Balboa Moon." Well, Trini lays the map in his lap and exclaims, "I can tell by the lay of the land, it's Lapland." Just then, the English wag, Sir Francis Duck, with his D. A. slicked and his pistol clicked, swoops down to announce, "The Armada is ours." And that's the end of the story.

LAW: What's the theme?

CHOO-CHOO: Don't give up the ship.

LAW: That's not a theme.

CHOO-CHOO: OK. It's our mada. I told you you wouldn't like it.

FERDINAND: That's not our old Columbus routine.

LAW (*aside to* TAL YO-YO): It's beginning to add up. Everything fits. The pieces of the jigsaw puzzle are all here. Get the picture?

TAL YO-YO (*aside to* LAW): Give them enough rope and the bough will break.

LAW: Justice Justice, excuse me, we'd very much like to see this Christopher Columbus routine. Especially if Ferdinand and Isabella are in it.

CHOO-CHOO: That's preposterous. Bongo, let's do our old Africa bit.
> Bingo Bango Bongo
> I don't want to leave the Congo
> No no no no no no

FERDINAND: Isabella?

CHOO-CHOO: Bongo, Bongo.

FERDINAND: That's how it begins—"Don't beat me. I'm here, my Queen. Isabella."

LAW (*aside to* YO-YO): We got them where we want them, Yo-yo. They're caught in vice's vice.

CHOO-CHOO (*aside to* FERDINAND): Bongo, get me out of this and you can write your own ticket—parking, speeding, whatever you want.

Stop! Allow me to introduce this court's special investigator, Ferdinand "Bongo" Kknot. Yes, you guessed it, this court has not been negligent in its duties to get to the bottom of this case—it's almost empty anyway—so we can start a new case. Bongo, take the oath.

FERDINAND: I am not now nor have I ever been a member . . .

CHOO-CHOO: Not that oath.

FERDINAND: I swear to tell the whole truth and nothing but the truth so help me God.

CHOO-CHOO: Nicely done. Begin.

FERDINAND: All right. I'll begin. But, first let me say how delighted I am. I am delighted. Now I'll begin. The virgin path that led me to the murderer of infamous Isabella twisted, curved, and had great shoulders. No, that's another road. That's when she took the high and I took the low and she got the Scotch before me.

CHOO-CHOO: Continue.

FERDINAND: All right. I'll continue. But, first let me say before I forget. Before I forget. Now I'll continue. It was a high road and a low road and she got the Scotch before me.

CHOO-CHOO: You already said that.

FERDINAND: I thought if I said it again I might get the Scotch.

CHOO-CHOO: Go on.

FERDINAND: All right. I'll go on. But, first let me say I won't beat around the bush. Why beat around the bush if she's not in the bush anyway?

CHOO-CHOO: Why beat around the bush if she's not in the bush?

FERDINAND: Exactly.

CHOO-CHOO: Exactly.

FERDINAND: That's what I said.

CHOO-CHOO: That's what I said.

FERDINAND: Did you call dibbies on that echo?

CHOO-CHOO: That's all right. You take it.

FERDINAND: Dibbies! Thank you. Should I go on?

CHOO-CHOO: Not before you tell me where she was if she wasn't in the bush. Was she on the road with the Scotch?

FERDINAND: With the Scotch and the beer.

CHOO-CHOO: Anheuser-Busch?

FERDINAND: Fine. I'll tell her you asked. Should I go on?

CHOO-CHOO: After that one, you'd better hurry.

FERDINAND: But, first let me say before I go on.

CHOO-CHOO: Well?

FERDINAND: Just wanted to hear if you were listening. The body of
Isabella Borgward was stashed in a nearby bush. To prevent the stealing of the body, I directed the local policeman to walk his beat around the bush. When I returned to
the bush however, the body was gone. I'll bust that cop to
the bush leagues, I thought. But where was he? And then
it hit me. Isabella loved gorillas. Could it be this cop was
her Bushman? Could it be, I dove further, that Isabella
was not dead at all? Could it be, I plunged still again, that
in an attempt to escape her life and start anew, she had
masqueraded her death with Bushman's help? Drowning
in this sea of thought, going down for the third time, I was
thrown a lifesaver by the only person that could have
saved me. The only person who knew the secret of Isabella Borgward. That person is you, Choo-Choo, you
threw me that lifesaver.

CHOO-CHOO: Is it a crime to carry candy?

FERDINAND: And what's more, you are Isabella Borgward!

Various states of shock from the others as CHOO-CHOO *puts on his*
ISABELLA *wig and trains a toy shotgun on them all.*

CHOO-CHOO: You're right, Bongo, but you'll never get me.

FERDINAND: You'll never make it, Choo-Choo, you're wanted in
fifty states for costuming outside the union.

CHOO-CHOO: Don't needle me, you sew-and-sew. I'll bare your
threads. I'll have you in stitches before the zigzag zugs.
Suzy, we're taking the first train out which happens to be
this one right here. I'll ride shotgun and you pedal.

*And off they go, toygunning it. The rest yell "After them!" and run
after them. The chase goes on.*

SUZY and CHOO-CHOO *have temporarily escaped and are discovered by
us. They are drinking.*

CHOO-CHOO: It's no use, Suzy. They'll get me sooner or later. This
is no life for a drunk like you, running away from the law,

never knowing where the next shot's coming from. What you need is a dependable fellow to bring home the Cold Duck. Why don't you marry a bartender, settle down and raise stools. Get yourself a little blue heaven with mahogany pinball machines, a little sawdust to temper the vomit, that old Monroe calendar with James himself in the nude. There's a life for you, Suzy, a rail to hang on. With peanuts for lunch, Slim Jims for dinner. Ah Suzy, you'll be dead in a year.

SUZY: All these years, Choo-Choo, I thought you were Isabella.

CHOO-CHOO: So did I, Suzy, until one day I said, "Take off that wig, you dumb broad. You're not Izzy." And there I was. Ain'tzy. I mean Choo-Choo. A new me. But, it wasn't long I doubted the new me was me. Maybe the real me was she. Ah yes, she the she-me was the real me. But, I didn't like me being she. Me didn't either. So me and I talked of killing she. Me and I couldn't agree more on killing she, but how we could agree less on how I knew not. But I did know Kknot. Tho' me knew Kknot not. I and me would trick Kknot into thinking she was dead. And you know the rest.

SUZY: Even if you had tricked Kknot into thinking she-you was dead, she-you wouldn't have been dead. It would have been a trick, which means that she-you does not not exist, does it not?

CHOO-CHOO: You've solved a knotty problem, Suzy. Now, what about the Kknotty problem?

SUZY: I don't know that, but I do know this. You're either Izzy or you're Ain'tzy.

CHOO-CHOO: What if I'm both?
(*Singing*)
    Iz I Izzy or iz I Ain'tzy or iz I both?
    Iz I Izzy or iz I Ain'tzy—I'll take an oath
    I don't know!

SUZY (*operatically*):
    I don't know!

CHOO-CHOO:

> I'd like to have a baby
> A lass or a little laddie
> But when it saw its mommy
> Wouldn't it say "daddy"?
>
> But don't you call me neuter
> I may be one
> I may be the other
> But one thing's sure
> If you call me "mister"
> You're talking to a sister
> Who's my brother!

Which goes to show . . . I don't know . . . what I'd show
. . . if I showed it . . .

SUZY (*passionately*):

> I don't know!

CHOO-CHOO:

> I don't know!

SUZY *and* CHOO-CHOO:

> They don't know!

The rest of the company enters and sings with Suzy.

CHORUS:

> Iz she Izzy or iz he Ain'tzy or iz they both?
> Iz she Izzy or iz he Ain'tzy—they'll take an oath
> They don't know
> They don't know!

CHOO-CHOO:

> Can't I be a she
> If I'm a he
> And still be me?
> He needs she
> Her needs him
> And I needs me
> Take your picks
> I are six!

CHORUS (*breathlessly*):
>He
>She
>Her
>Him
>I
>Me
>Wee!
>Iz she Izzy or iz he Ain'tzy or: Am they six?
>Iz she Izzy or iz he Ain'tzy or: Am they six?

The above is repeated chorally as the following is sung individually:
>Iz she Izzy
>Iz he Ain'tzy
>Iz her Izzy
>Iz him Ain'tzy

CHOO-CHOO:
>Ain't I Izzy or
>Iz me Ain'tzy

ALL:

>Or am they six
>Or iz they both
>Or six
>Or both
>Or six
>Both
>Six
>Both
>Both
>Iz
>They
>Both!?!

"SKIN"

And somebody's
out to kill me.

"TRI-GAM"

a la fraternity; Player Piano

36   LONNIE CARTER

40

LONNIE CARTER

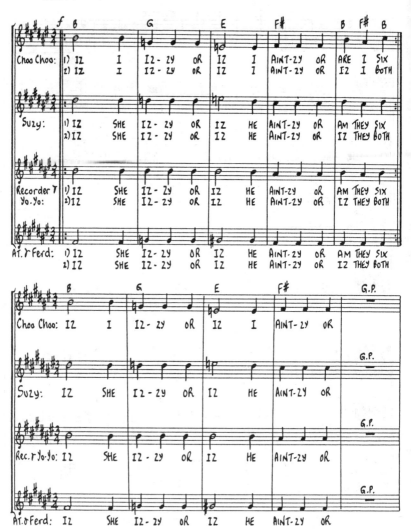

Slow (Piano Silent)

Waiting for G

FIRST PERFORMANCE:
November 1973, Yale Repertory Theatre, New Haven, Connecticut

Jonathan Marks as Rebozzo
Alvin Epstein as Lickie

Directed by Isaiah Shefter
With nods to Samuel Beckett

THE PLAYERS:

REBOZZO
LICKIE

Alvin Epstein as Lickie
(Photograph by William Baker)

REBOZZO & LICKIE. REBOZZO holds the rope around LICKIE's neck.

REBOZZO: Think, pig!

LICKIE: Given the existence as uttered forth in the public polls of Galloping and Harris of an unpopular President quaquaquaqua with heavy jowls quaquaquaqua above law and order who from the heights monarchical neglect loves all his American children dearly with some exceptions for reasons known perfectly clear and suffers like the divine monarch with those crises in multiples of six which for reasons known perfectly partly cloudy timidity index zero plunges self in torment and lust over My Lai not withstanding calleys on clemency writing fingers William Callous not withstanding blister on trigger finger gooks dinks quacks quack doctors at Bach Mai thus the strafing thereof thereupon for reasons perfectly zonked striving to save the hamlet by destroying the hamlet inasmuch as warification in addition to plunging self in rage public enemy number Dean must be gangbusted remind self to have wet dream giving hickey to Maureen concurrently simultaneously not having Ziegler to shove around anymore according to the works of Niccolo Stans and Maurice Mitchiavelli tentatively titled From Prince to Pauper in one greasy Vesco considering the Logorrhea of one Spirochete Agnococcus by and large perfectly obfuscatory since the death of General Eisenminute in light of the labors of Scammon and Wattenberg I resume my solitary drinking but not so fast gather the wagons around the Rose Garden and let the chips and arrows of outrageous something or another plop where they may as I resume shaking the Quakers shaking down entire communities select colleges shittier than Whittier where sat I picking kicking my clubfootballs on the other hand with regard to the other hand sitting in Sedan Chair II fondling the red and black checkers three pieces to the King Lickie III keep your wits Ulasewicz about you am I my brother's bugger for reasons perfectly opaque the facts are there get thee behind me Watergate Water Satan plunging self in spite for reasons imperfectly hazy I resume toughing it out when the going gets bunctious the bunctious get going in spite of the labors lost of Baldeman and Dichlich I resume my solitary

47

drinking but not so slow I resume establishing beyond one doubt there is more joy in the Ovum Office over the castration of one long-haired conspirator than over 99 H.R. "Bob's" who never had any balls at all take that Uncle Sam and ram it up your Archibald Cock a conspiracy of one one hand clapping other holding slogan hire thugs smash him right in his sign off fire in the EOB color of ketchup on cottage cheese blast out of the water the bench-warmer's game plan then CREEP into Gemstone rifle Elkikesberg's psykiketrist rifle but not so fast forgetting the tape on the door for reasons known perfectly cloudy zero per cent chance of humility that is to say plumbing the depths of my executive privy privylege privilege looking for my comb out plumbs G. Gordon Giggy chomping soggy Havana stogie sailing the shitten waves of yachty Miami making all call girls suck sugar cane suck I am singer sewing up twat Helen Gahagan Douglas Alger Alger no Algernon Ssssssss this too shall pass water pass gate collect $200,000 get 'em Egil eat crow you mutha Hunt at the Buckley bosom tainting the evidentiary tree in spite of the football the facts the tackles are there end sweep end mine sweep I resume alas alas abandoned unfinished insofar as in spite for Attorney-Buck Private Brahmin Bastardson no son of Richard all alone by my telephone sterile organizing the plane crash Mrs. H's payments lost forever to telephonic contact whereas executive clemency for Sammy Nigger Jr. who once brushed Trixie's tit he no spook just glass-eyed fascist folk met him on the George Washington Freeway sent greetings to crooner Sin Sin Sin Hatera guinea wopupon whereupon his 9th toupee fell onto the 18th tee picked up and fondled by Hoffa's team players Colson to take truth-detector test in light of laborious lies in so far as in spite of the Redskins' security makes San David Grand Clemente Key Cay Camp Bisquay Bisc-eye I want a water biscuit with mustard all homes less valuable money money Rebozzo Reclown the cheat ethic dollars Abplap Abplop Abadabbaplopplap Planalp . . . Aerosol . . . unfinished . . .

LICKIE *is silent.*

The Sovereign State
of Boogedy Boogedy

FIRST PERFORMANCE:
March 1985, Victory Gardens Theatre, Chicago, Illinois

Sam Sanders as Abed-nego
Ed Wheeler as Shadrach
Sephus Booker as Meshach
Candace Taylor as Danielle
Larry Venson as Nebuchadnezzar
Vicky George as The Fourth Man

Directed by Dennis Zacek

THE PLAYERS:

ABED-NEGO
SHADRACH
MESHACH
DANIELLE
NEBUCHADNEZZAR
THE FOURTH MAN

THE SCENE:
A Court of Law

LEFT TO RIGHT: Sam Sanders as Abed-nego; Ed Wheeler as Shadrach; Sephus Booker as Meshach
(Photograph by Jennifer Girard)

ACT ONE

Darkest stage. A spot hits ABED-NEGO'S *face.*

ABED-NEGO: I can't find her. Morning 8 a.m. Not beside me. Not below. The other little girl asleep. I shake her. "Where is Eva?" She doesn't know. She falls back asleep. I smell my fingers. Twelve years old. She filled my hand with her smell. Miami. Thirty-six hours aboard this train and Miami will be ours. Where is Eva? Why did I agree? Be ashamed! Of what? It's just, I said. It's just what, she said. It's Just-tice, I said. It's just this, she said, I slept above, I swear, your Honor. I kissed them both goodnight. I am asleep. I hear my name, my new name, the name she has given me. "Bobka, I am coming up to you." She is in my compartment. I feel her feet though I do not touch them. Size 5, no more. Her calves strong, hairless. Her thighs, I cannot see. I stop. She proffers a book. Medieval. Oriental. Pornography. My career passes before me. It is over. It is after me. An eye for an eye. My sex for a tooth. I want her teeth. In the book, lances arrows enter women. The women contain them. She pulls up my knee. She strides my knee. She rides. To speak the truth. Voir dire, your Honor. I smell her. She puts her hand to herself and then to my lips. I eat. Aching, I. She takes me in her hands, stops, then gives me back to myself. "Here, you take it." She laughs. Then I force her. Or does she force me?

The spot expands. The stage fills with light. ABED-NEGO *in judge's robes.* HE *puts on his judge's wig and exits. The stage to black. We hear a man singing "Iz You Iz Or Iz You Ain't Mah Baby." Lights up on* SHADRACH, *in full judgly garb but sans wig add railroad cap, wheeling* HIMself *in on a flat car.*

SHADRACH:

> Pardon me, boys
> I' dat de Chabanooba Choo Choo
> Track 29
> Boy you can gib me a shine
>
> Ah'd like to hab a baby
> A lass or a little laddie

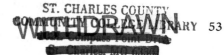

But when it saw its mommy
Wouldn't it say "Daddy"

Iz you iz
Or iz you ain't
Mah baby

Ah, say dere, Princefish, does de name o' Rubah Begonyah
ring a bell

Iz you iz
Or iz you ain't
Mah baby

Judge Solomon Skybumskybum has ruled dat de fathah is
de chile to de man. In de appellate procedyah, Justice Choo-
Choo Justice has found dat de man is de chile to de fathah.
In de suuperior court o' de firs' districk o' de Districk o' de
gem o' de Ocean Judge Jud Judge has declared dat de chile
is de fathah to de man. In de suupremest body o' de most
exalted division o' de Prime Movah o' all Poobahs i' de
liberated emirate o' Boogedy-Boogedy Justice Leaner Hot
Dog has decreed dat de man is de fathah to de chile.

A bell rings.

Does de name o' Rubah Begonyah ring a bell?

Iz you iz
Or iz you ain't
Mah baby

Ah'd like to hab a baby
A lass or a little laddie
But when it saw its mommy
Wouldn't it say "Daddy"

Pardon me boys
I' dat de Chabanooba Choo Choo
Track 29
Boy . . . are you mah boy
Boy . . . are you my boy
—Dr. Pullmotah, may Ah hab a word wid you?
—Sorry, son, Ah'm in fo' a hard day o' labah in de
    paternity ward.
—Son? You called me Son?

Boy . . . you . . . can . . . gib . . . me . . . a . . . shine . . . boy
. . . iz you mah boy?
Justice Feline Braunschweiger has decided

Lights start to fade.

i' de uppest halls o' Justice Blindness dat de muthafrigger
he not only NOT de fathah o' de chile he not de man
eidder.

> Iz you iz
> Or iz you ain't
> Mah baby

Lights are out. Up on MESHACH, *in traditional judge's robes and wig.*

MESHACH: Everything is true and false. A merchant goes bank-
rupt. He sends his son to a wealthy man who may or may
not owe him a favor. The man is known for his hauteur
and keeps the son three days waiting. When he finally
grants the audience, he deigns not to look at the youth,
who, growing impatient, speaks. "Sire, my father you
know. He has lost his wealth and sent me to you to beg a
loan of three camels laden with silver so that he might
once again be prosperous." "Out of my sight, worm!", says
the man. As the son leaves, the servants of the man give
him the reins of 30 camels laden with silver. The merchant deals wisely and becomes rich beyond his dreams.
"Go to the wealthy man, my son, and return him three-
fold what he has given us." The son obeys, but the man's
hauteur is more extreme than before. "Be gone, cretin,
you do not understand hauteur and generosity." Everything is true and false.

Lights out on MESHACH. *Lights up on a courtroom.* DANIELLE, *a lawyer.*

DANIELLE: All rise for the honorable Judges Shadrach, Meshach
and Abed-nego.

The three Judges enter and take their positions.

ABED-NEGO: Call King Nebuchadnezzar to take the oath before
the Court.

DANIELLE: The Court calls King Nebuchadnezzar.

NEBUCHADNEZZAR *enters in kingly robe.*

DANIELLE (*with Good Book extended*): Do you solemnly swear . . .

ABED-NEGO: Will the witness place his right hand on the Good Book extended?

DANIELLE: Do you solemnly swear . . .

ABED-NEGO: Will the witness do as directed or be cited in contempt of court?

DANIELLE: Give me your right hand.

SHE parts his robe, then throws it open.

DANIELLE: A strait jacket! Your Honors, not one hour ago my client was unbound.

ABED-NEGO: He is not *your* client. That implies an adversary relationship with the Court. That is not what you have. You are here merely to advise the client.

DANIELLE: The what?

ABED-NEGO: *The* client, not *your* client. He is the client, the ward, if you will, of the state.

SHADRACH: Dese n' dose distinckshuns distinkly distink if you gittin' mah draft n' if you ain't den git me i' de bottle fo' Ah die frob dry, yeh hunnggga hunnggga . . .

ABED-NEGO: The distinction is this. Call him what you will . . .

SHADRACH: What you will.

ABED-NEGO: But know that he is not to be defended, only presented.

DANIELLE: Beside the point. Binding him as if he were a dangerous psychotic is patently illegal.

SHADRACH: Ah's heard o' de bald eagle, but de ill-eagle, dat's a mighty sick bird. You say you got a patent on dis disease? Ah'm callin de U. S. Reg. Pat. Off.

HE pulls out a toy phone.

Hello, Reggie?

ABED-NEGO: He is a dangerous *felon* and needs restraining.

DANIELLE: Felon, you call him! The man has not yet been tried. Judge Abed-nego, I demand you remove yourself from this case.

ABED-NEGO: Disqualify myself? Never!

MESHACH: Tilt.

ABED-NEGO: Not even if I have tilted. This pinball remains.

MESHACH: Pinhead. How many angels can dance on the ball of a pin?

DANIELLE: Judge Meshach, may I get a ruling?

MESHACH: Why do hummingbirds hum?

DANIELLE: Because they've forgotten the words.

MESHACH: Release the prisoner.

DANIELLE takes off his robe and unbinds HIM. HE *growls at* HER.

DANIELLE: Stop your growling. You're being tried for the most serious crimes. Don't make it harder on yourself. Please keep calm.

HE *stops growling.* DANIELLE *once more extends the Good Book.*

Do you solemnly swear . . .

ABED-NEGO: Your right hand.

NEBUCHADNEZZAR *puts his right hand on the Good Book, throws it down and stomps on it.* HE *stops.*

DANIELLE: It is the Good Book, your Honors, but it is not his.

ABED-NEGO: This shall be added to the list of charges.

DANIELLE: Gentlemen, is not one of the charges that this King tried to impose his religion on those with different beliefs? If he is forced to swear on *our* Bible, would not we be open to the same charge?

MESHACH: Why is it that men are not such sots as they were in days of yore?

DANIELLE: We are no longer indefatigable topers.

MESHACH: The charge is dropped. Proceed, Judge Abed-nego.

ABED-NEGO (*reading*):   The charges are as follows: "Nebuchadnezzar the King made an image of gold, whose height was
threescore cubits . . . "

SHADRACH: Threescore dat Cupid, hey? He doin shitten well for
hisself he shot an arrow he knew damn well where and it
landed in de middle o' dis burnin birdbush right where dey
loves it.

ABED-NEGO: " . . . and the breadth thereof six cubits."

SHADRACH: Six Cupids scorin three times Ah's confused tho Ah
duz right fine mahselfs shack-up Shadrach shack in the
rack.

ABED-NEGO: "He set it up in the plain of Dura, in the province of
Babylon."

SHADRACH: Abed-nego. Dat's a-bed-nego nega to bed nigga a bad
niggah ah's a bad niggah . . .

ABED-NEGO: "Then Nebuchadnezzar the King sent to gather together the satraps . . . "

SHADRACH: Satraps Meshachs and Abed-neggahs.

ABED-NEGO: " . . . the deputies and the governors, the judges the
treasurers the counsellors the sheriffs . . . "

SHADRACH: On Comet on Cupid on Donner on Blitzen.

ABED-NEGO: " . . . and all the rulers of the provinces to come to the
dedication of the image which Nebuchadnezzar the King
had set up. Then the satraps . . . "

SHADRACH: Satraps satraps dem dry traps . . .

ABED-NEGO: " . . . the deputies and the governors, the judges and
the treasurers, the counsellors the sheriffs . . . "

SHADRACH: Ah passes.

ABED-NEGO: " . . . and all the rulers of the provinces were gathered
together unto the dedication of the image that Nebuchadnezzar the King had set up."

SHADRACH (*sing-song*): . . . the image that Nebuchadnezzar the King had set up.

ABED-NEGO: "And they stood before the image . . . "

SHADRACH: . . . that Nebuchadnezzar the King had set up.

ABED-NEGO: " . . . that Nebuchadnezzar the King had set up."

SHADRACH: Tatatatatatatatatatata

> *SHADRACH breaks into an Irish jig. For a moment ABED-NEGO gets caught up in the dance.*

ABED-NEGO (*having stopped*): Irish jig.

SHADRACH: Yuk yuk yuk

DANIELLE: Judge Meshach, may we hear the rest of the charge?

> *NEBUCHADNEZZAR growls.*

Your headaches will be worse. You will not dream. Then I cannot tell you what your dreams portend.

> *HE stops growling.*

MESHACH: Portend you are green and wear a mask. What are you?

DANIELLE: The Lone Lime.

MESHACH: Let us hear the rest of the charge.

ABED-NEGO: "Then the herald cried aloud . . ."

SHADRACH: Mah daddy's name was Harold.

ABED-NEGO: ". . . to you it is commanded, o peoples, nations and languages, that at what time ye hear the sound of the cornet, flute, harp, sackbut . . ."

SHADRACH: De sackbutt, say hey?

ABED-NEGO: "Psaltery . . ."

SHADRACH: Peppery.

ABED-NEGO: ". . . and all kinds of music . . ."

SHADRACH: Wid de spoons on de cheeks n' de sacks on de butts, baby, you n' me gonna exhume Major Bowes.

ABED-NEGO: "Ye fall down and worship the golden image that Nebuchadnezzar the King hath set up."

SHADRACH: One mo' time.

ABED-NEGO: "And whoso falleth not down and worshippeth shall the same hour be cast into the midst of a burning fiery furnace."

NEBUCHADNEZZAR growls. DANIELLE stares HIM to silence.

SHADRACH (*professorially*): Herodotus speaks of a great golden statue of Zeus in the temple of Belus in Babylon and Nestle in the Marginalia reminds us of the mention in Ammianus Marcellinus of a colossal golden statue erected by Antiochus Epiphanes in the temple of Daphne at Antioch.

MESHACH: Really? I mean, really.

SHADRACH: And you thought Ah just one mo' hung snowball.

ABED-NEGO: I will now continue with the prosecution.

DANIELLE: Objection, your Honors, if an adversary relationship does not exist in this court, if the King is not *my* client, if I am not his *defense* attorney, neither you nor anyone else can *prosecute*.

ABED-NEGO: "And whoso falleth not down and worshippeth shall the same hour be cast into the midst of a burning fiery furnace."

NEBUCHADNEZZAR growls.

DANIELLE (*staring HIM to silence*): I will have an answer to my question!

ABED-NEGO: One more outburst and the ape's teeth will be wired shut.

DANIELLE: An answer!

SHADRACH: Why is a woman like a frying pan?

MESHACH snaps a switchblade under SHADRACH's chin.

DANIELLE: I'm sure I don't know.

SHADRACH: Ah withdraws de question.

MESHACH: Continue the reading of the charge.

DANIELLE: Let the record show the unanswered objection.

MESHACH: What record?

DANIELLE: I can't answer that.

MESHACH: Let the record show that the attorney has refused to answer.

ABED-NEGO: "Therefore at that time, when all the peoples heard the sound of the cornet flute harp sackbut psaltery and all kinds of music, all the people the nations and the languages fell down and worshipped the golden image that Nebuchadnezzar the King had set up."

DANIELLE: Objection. The charges, not the entire account as we have it from the Book of Daniel.

ABED-NEGO: Overruled. The scene must be set.

DANIELLE: Simply, what is the charge against this man?

DANIELLE snatches a document from a court table and reads.

"Nebuchadnezzar who calls himself King . . ."

ABED-NEGO: Counsel is out of order.

DANIELLE: I object to the statement in the charge, who *calls* himself King.

ABED-NEGO: Will counsel cease and desist?

NEBUCHADNEZZAR: KNRI—King Nebuchadnezzar Rex Judaeorum.

ABED-NEGO: He claims to be Babylonian, but he quotes Latin. He is a tool of the Romans and nothing more.

NEBUCHADNEZZAR: KNRI—Koffin Nails Running In.

DANIELLE: The implication is that he calls himself King as do no others, when in fact all Babylon recognized him as sovereign.

MESHACH: Babylon no longer exists.

DANIELLE: He may call himself what he wishes.

MESHACH: He may call himself what he wishes.

SHADRACH: What he wishes.

DANIELLE (*reading*): "Nebuchadnezzar is charged with willfully directing the three known as Shadrach Meshach and Abednego to be placed in the fiery furnace and there to be consumed as punishment for refusal to bow down before the golden idol. Charge 2: Nebuchadnezzar is charged . . .

SHADRACH: Hunnggga hunnggga hold it, sweet mah basil, you is extendin beyon' de boun' o' justiticial proprietude. Ah means n' Ah mean what Ah says, da's mine, boobie, nice ones you got, fine on de uppah's dere, de lift iz not all hunnggga hunnggga positibely patrician, Patricia, Ah say dere . . .

MESHACH: Ah say dere, I mean, the second charge belongs to Shadrach. Abed-nego will finish before he will begin.

ABED-NEGO: I'll not finish before I begin, thank you.

MESHACH: You're welcome.

DANIELLE: No matter what the crime, the same meal's served to all.

ABED-NEGO: "Wherefore at that time certain Chaldeans came near and brought accusation against the Jews. They answered and said to Nebuchadnezzar the King, O King, live forever."

MESHACH: No matter what the crime, the same meal's served to all.

ABED-NEGO: May I ask my leanéd and hungryed colleague to refrain?

MESHACH: Ah, yes of course.

ABED-NEGO: "Thou, o King, hast made a decree . . ."

MESHACH (*not fooling, off somewhere*): Of course, the course is the same for us all.

ABED-NEGO: "That every man that shall hear the sound of the cornet flute harp sackbut psaltery and dulcimer and all kinds of music shall fall down and worship the golden image."

MESHACH (*still off*): What do people never eat at breakfast?

DANIELLE: Lunch and dinner.

ABED-NEGO: "And whoso falleth not down and worshippeth shall be cast into the midst of a burning fiery furnace."

SHADRACH: You may tell me to go to hell, but Ah ain't nevah goin' back to Missippissi da's M-i-s-s-i-p-p-i-s-s-i.

ABED-NEGO: "There are certain Jews whom thou hast appointed over the affairs of the province of Babylon—Shadrach, Meshach and Abed-nego."

SHADRACH, MESHACH & ABED-NEGO:
>We are the boys of furnace
>We grew up in Judea
>We sapped the milk and honey stands
>We've never more been freea
>Then to our land came old King Nebuch
>With eunuchs and Chaldeans
>He snatched us off to Babylon
>Like slaves not human beins

What follows is simultaneously presented.

ABED-NEGO: To see to speak, voir dire, your Honor, I smelled her. She put her hand to herself and then to my lips. I ate. Aching, I was. She took me in her hands, stopped, then gave me back to myself. "Here you take it." She laughed. Then I forced her. Or did she force me?

SHADRACH:
>Iz you iz
>Or iz you ain't
>Mah baby
>Pardon me, boys
>I' dat de Chabanooba Choo-Choo
>Track 29
>Boy, you can give me a shine
>Dr. Pullmotor, may Ah hab a word wid you?
>Sorry, son, but Ah'm in fo' a hard day o' labor i' de
>   paternity ward.
>Son?

MESHACH: Everything is true and false. Everything is true and false. Everything is true and false Everything is true and false everything is trueandfalseeverythingistrueandfalse.

THEY stop together. THEY are soundlessly embarrassed at this loss of control. THEY gather themselves.

MESHACH: Judge Abed-nego shall procede.

ABED-NEGO: "These men, o King, have not regarded thee; they serve not thy gods, nor worship the golden image which thou has set up."

MESHACH: If Beauty's in the eye of the beholder . . .

DANIELLE: Truth is in the pupil somewhere too.

ABED-NEGO: "Then Nebuchadnezzar in *his* rage and fury commanded to bring Shadrach Meshach and Abed-nego."

DANIELLE: Objection. Rage and fury is an interpretation. *His* rage and fury is further interpretation.

ABED-NEGO: This is how the text reads.

DANIELLE: What text?

ABED-NEGO: The Book of Daniel.

DANIELLE: May I once again point out that the Court should present the charges only, not an embellished scenario.

ABED-NEGO: You are telling the Court how to conduct?

DANIELLE: I am.

MESHACH: She is.

SHADRACH: High-heel sneakah.

MESHACH & DANIELLE: We beg your pardon.

SHADRACH: Beg it, baby. Put on your high-heel sneakahs 'cause Ah'll be down to get ya in a pushcart, Becky, bettah be ready 'bout half past eight, now Becky don' be late . . .

ABED-NEGO: "Then they brought these men before the King."

SHADRACH: We're gonna be there when the band starts playin!

MESHACH: May I call you Shad or Mr. Rach?

SHADRACH: Call me Sir.

ABED-NEGO: "Nebuchadnezzar answered and said unto them . . ."

NEBUCHADNEZZAR: Is it of purpose, o Shadrach Meshach and Abed-nego that ye serve not my god nor worship the golden image which I have set up?

DANIELLE: Stop.

NEBUCHADNEZZAR: Now if ye be ready at what time ye hear the sound of the cornet flute harp sackbut psaltery and dulcimer and all kinds of music, ye fall down and worship the image which I have set up, well.

DANIELLE: May I ask the Court for a short recess?

SHADRACH: Recess! Goodie gumshoes, Ah's playin "Ring Roun' De Rosy Begonia." Jus' fit yore ring roun' mah rosy begonia, as de bishop said to de actress.

NEBUCHADNEZZAR: But if ye worship not, ye shall be cast the same hour into the midst of a burning fiery furnace and who is that god that shall deliver you out of my hands?

ABED-NEGO: "Shadrach Meshach and Abed-Nego answered and said to the King:"

SHADRACH, MESHACH & ABED-NEGO: O, Nebuchadnezzar, we have no need to answer thee in this matter. For our God whom we serve is able to deliver us from the burning fiery furnace and if he wishes he will deliver us out of thine hand, o King. But if it is not His will, be it known unto thee, o King, that we will not serve thy gods, nor worship the golden image which thou hast set up.

DANIELLE: Your Honors, is it not clear that your special involvement in this case demands that you disqualify yourselves?

ABED-NEGO: Who better to try one's enemy than oneself?

SHADRACH: We hab seen de enema n' he iz thru us ober n' out.

DANIELLE: Judge Meshach, is it not clear?

MESHACH: If your enemy prospers, do not be vexed, but even pray on his behalf that he may prosper to the full.

NEBUCHADNEZZAR *is calm throughout the following.*

ABED-NEGO: "Then was Nebuchadnezzar full of fury and the form of his visage was charged against Shadrach Meshach and Abed-nego."

DANIELLE: I want to know why a woman is like a frying pan.

ABED-NEGO: "Therefore he spake:

NEBUCHADNEZZAR *does not speak.*

"Therefore he spake."

NEBUCHADNEZZAR *does not speak.*

Will counsel instruct the defendant?

DANIELLE: The what?

ABED-NEGO: The King.

DANIELLE: The what?

ABED-NEGO: Speak, snake.

DANIELLE: I will not allow this man to suffer more abuse.

ABED-NEGO: What do you propose to do about it?

SHADRACH: Ah proposes molasses toasts wid de El Monico white port to drown me all down.

DANIELLE: A change of venue.

SHADRACH: If'n Ah duzn't hab me a booze n' watah chaser hol' de watah, Ah's a goosed cook widout no paddle.

MESHACH *hands* SHADRACH *a flask.* SHADRACH *loves it and gulps from it.* MESHACH *takes it back.*

ABED-NEGO: Motion denied. Where would be this new venue?

DANIELLE: Proceed.

ABED-NEGO: The Court directs counsel to answer. Where would be this new venue?

DANIELLE: The motion has been denied.

ABED-NEGO & SHADRACH: Answer.

DANIELLE: I have none. Had none in mind. The case must be heard here now before you three.

NEBUCHADNEZZAR: I command that the furnace be heated seven times more than it is wont to be heated. I further command certain mighty men in my army to bind Shadrach Meshach and Abed-nego *and* (my emphasis) to cast them into the burning fiery furnace.

ABED-NEGO: "Then these men were bound in their hosen their tunics and their mantles and their other garments and were cast into the midst of the burning fiery."

SHADRACH: Furnace.

ABED-NEGO: The Court calls time-out.

DANIELLE: Does the Court rest?

ABED-NEGO: Time-out.

SHADRACH: Shadrach, he's our man, if he can't do it Meshach can. Meshach, he's our man, if he can't do it Abed-nego can. Abed-nego, he's our man, if he can't do it the team can. Yea team yea team yea!

SHADRACH produces an ABA basketball and starts passing it around. ALL make a circle and do the Globetrotter bit, whistling "Sweet Georgia Brown" with SHADRACH singing it. Then the Trotter baseball routine with SHADRACH as batter.

Enuf dis henanigans, Ah's goin' back to playin' brown ball, as de actress said to de honky.

ABED-NEGO: Time-in.

ALL scramble into Court positions with the energy of musical chairs.

DANIELLE: You can't have your cake and eat it too.

MESHACH: If you fall between two stools.

DANIELLE (*she is not reading*): "Therefore because the king's commandment was urgent and the furnace exceeding hot the flame of the fire slew those men that took up Shadrach Meshach and Abed-nego."

ABED-NEGO: Verify your statements please.

DANIELLE: I quote from the same account, your Honor, the Book of Daniel. You saw fit to leave off at the crucial point, but no matter, I will complete the picture.

ABED-NEGO: How is it you have the same account as I?

DANIELLE: How is it? It's just fine, o Justice.

SHADRACH (*screaming*): AH WANTS MAH MONEY!

DANIELLE: "And these three men Shadrach Meshach and Abed-nego fell down bound into the midst of the burning fiery furnace."

SHADRACH: Dat was George C. Scott in De Hus'lah.

DANIELLE: "Then Nebuchadnezzar the King was astonied . . ."

SHADRACH: A-st<u>o</u>nied. Ah asmokin n' atokin.

HE inhales deeply.

But Ah ain't no token you call me token Ah gonna charco' your apartheid.

DANIELLE: " . . . and rose up in haste. He spake and said unto his counsellors:"

SHADRACH: Uhuru!

MESHACH: Do you know the joke about Japanese cream?

SHADRACH: Man, can't say as to Ah has or as to Ah hasn't as to Ah hasn't can't say nohow.

MESHACH: Know-how, good old American.

ABED-NEGO: May we?

NEBUCHADNEZZAR: Did not we cast three men bound into the midst of the fire?

DANIELLE: "They answered and said unto the King:"

NEBUCHADNEZZAR: Lo, I see four men loose, walking in the midst of the fire and they have no hurt and the aspect of the fourth is like a son of the gods.

SHADRACH (*singing*): O-o-o yes I'm the Great Pretender.

MESHACH & ABED-NEGO form behind SHADRACH in song line. During the presentation by DANIELLE & NEBUCHADNEZZAR, THEY will do with total authenticity "The Great Pretender" by the Platters. The two camps vie for our attention.

DANIELLE: "Then Nebuchadnezzar came to the mouth of the burning fiery furnace. He spake and said:"

NEBUCHADNEZZAR: Shadrach Meshach and Abed-nego, ye servants of the most high God, come forth and come hither.

DANIELLE: "Then Shadrach Meshach and Abed-nego came forth out of the midst of the fire. And the satraps the deputies and the governors and the King's counsellors being gathered together saw these men, that the fire had no power upon their bodies nor was the hair of their heads singed, neither were their hosen changed, nor had the smell of fire passed on them. Nebuchadnezzar spake and said:"

NEBUCHADNEZZAR: Blessed be the God of Shadrach Meshach and Abed-nego who hath sent his angel and delivered his servants that trusted in him and have changed the King's word and have yielded their bodies that they might not serve or worship any god except their own God. Therefore I make a decree that every people nation and language which speak anything amiss against the God of Shadrach Meshach and Abed-nego shall be cut in pieces and their houses shall be made a dunghill, because there is no other God that is able to deliver after this sort.

The JUDGES finish their song as NEBUCHADNEZZAR finishes declaiming. Now the light is on HIM only. HE begins to recount.

I am steering a car around a circular driveway of fine gravel. The mechanism is defective making the turn hard. A woman in an off-white pleated night-gown stands in the way thirty feet around the curve. I keep slowing. The slower I drive the harder it is to turn. She sees me. I do not think to touch the horn. She does not move. If she remains, she will be hit. Ever so slowly. I turn the wheel more than before but the wheel does not turn as much as before. I will hit her I will hate her I will sob I will want to love her. I let go the wheel. My arms are loose, I close my eyes, the car stops.

STOP.

I am in a stadium filled with people watching an event. From the other side of the field someone is throwing pencils in my direction as if they are darts. It is not known for certain who, if anyone in particular, the thrower is aiming at. The pencils come in a continual flurry driving all of us away from our seats. Then it becomes clear. I move to the right, everyone else to the left. A woman wearing an enormous hat held on by a pin as large as a sabre is running at me, throwing the pencils at my forehead but never hitting. I leap over a wall and into a courtyard. At the other end in front of me is the woman. I close my eyes in surrender but I do not think that is what she wants.

The light expands to include DANIELLE.

DANIELLE: In the first dream you have control, but not enough. You can slow the car but not stop it altogether. The woman will not move out of the way. You want to hit her hate her sob and love her. You will do all those things, but first you must let go before you can have her. Remember, when you let go the wheel, the car stopped. In the second dream you seem to have no control. You are being attacked. No one will defend you; everyone moves away. The hatpin/sabre terrifies you. You try to run away. It doesn't matter to her. Both enrage her. That's how she lives. She is crying with love-hate for the hurt you and she have done to her. Give it up, pack it in. When you let go the wheel, the car stops.

Lights out. We go to SHADRACH, MESHACH & ABED-NEGO down and bound in the midst of the fiery furnace. A FOURTH MAN moves among THEM.

SHADRACH (*about the FOURTH who is untying HIM*): Who dis dude?

FOURTH MAN: M'man, don't ya knows me? Ah here's Richie the Itch.

SHADRACH: Well scratch my mouth, Richie m'man!

FOURTH MAN: Ah's springin' you, baby.

HE finishes untying HIM and moves to ABED-NEGO.

ABED-NEGO: Who are you?

FOURTH MAN: Don't you know me?

ABED-NEGO: Yes. No.

FOURTH MAN: I'm from the Legion.

ABED-NEGO: The Legion hates me.

FOURTH MAN: May our enemy prosper.

HE finishes untying ABED-NEGO *and moves to* MESHACH.

MESHACH: I don't want to be untied last. I don't want to be untied at all.

FOURTH MAN: Everyone will be untied.

MESHACH: I don't want it. I came here but I will not go.

FOURTH MAN: If you think you come or go, that is your delusion. Now accept this.

The THREE are now untied. As the FOURTH MAN disappears, the THREE speak in unison.

SHADRACH, MESHACH & ABED-NEGO: Praise the Lord!

SHADRACH: N' pass the amontillado!

The Fiery Furnace becomes the Courtroom. The JUDGES back in position. NEBUCHADNEZZAR & DANIELLE *before THEM.*

DANIELLE: Nebuchadnezzar is charged with forcing his religion on those who hold another God sacred. There is no doubt he did this and he seems to deserve punishment, but who among you will mete it out . . .

ABED-NEGO: I.

DANIELLE: When the Lord God on High did not see fit to destroy the King. In fact, your Honors, the Lord forgave him and the King prospered for many years after. Would you in the name of Justice pretend to do what the Lord would not? Are you saying the Lord is unjust?

MESHACH (*to* NEBUCHADNEZZAR): Do you wish to speak before I ask the question?

NEBUCHADNEZZAR *is silent and does not move.*

Very well. Are you guilty or not?

NEBUCHADNEZZAR *takes a flute from inside his robe. HE blows one note.*

Not.

End ACT ONE.

ACT TWO

ABED-NEGO: She is in a diner in a booth. She empties her purse of three vials, pink green and pink. A pink-smocked waitress approaches. She asks the woman to bring her another vial. The waitress refuses and begins a tantrum. She takes my hand and silently asks me to take her away. The waitress shouts. Trucks prevent us from crossing the street. We cross the wrong way. I ask her why she is barefoot. She tells me she could not find the proper shoes. Her steps are short but quick so she might catch up with me who holds her hand. Her head is a tomato with a flat side in back which I see in her profile. She repeatedly looks to the side to look at me as I not so gently pull her along. She is frightened. She smiles. We head for an apartment and a canopied bed I do not know. The spread is coarse under her back as I spin around her as she spins her legs around me. She loses consciousness. Her hair is sopping. The shower turns scalding. She is an idiot child. She swims around my tongue. My eyes are open. My skin loses its oil. "Come swimming with me," she says. I forget what the waitress shouted, but it was not relevant at all, your Honor, not at all. The next day we leave Miami. She does not speak to me on the train nor does she come to my bed. I spend two nights thinking I can feel the flat back of her head.

Lights down, then up for SHADRACH.

SHADRACH (*à la Louis Armstrong*):

> Pops, did you hear the story of Long John Dean
> A bold bank robber from Bowling Green
> Was sent to the jailhouse yesterday
> But late last night he made his getaway
> He was long gone from Kentucky
> Long gone ain't he lucky
> Long gone what Ah mean
> Long John Dean frob Bowling Green

Ah's be on a lekcha gig all's obah de bigra Nigra collegiums i' de deepes' down home. Ah goes to Frisk U. in Memphisk, Fiveessee, den Ah goes to George Washington Cardboard i' de Elephuntkegee Institute fo' Highah Earnin' specializin' i' Abribadabra Abriculcha n' LaBotany big on greens all de teache's grabbin' yub folk by de collards n' wringin' turkah necks 'til dey's gobbled de 101 abuses fo' de peanuts n' de miscegenation nuts discobered by G. W. Carpetbaggah.

> Long John stood on de railroad tie
> Waitin' fo' a freight train to come by
> Freight train come by puffin' n' flyin'
> Oughtta see Long John grabbin' dat fly
> He was long gone
> Frob Kentucky
> Long gone
> Ain't he lucky
> Long gone
> What Ah mean
> Long Gone John frob Bowling Green

N' Ah's lekchain' n' groobin' Ah'm i' de groob wid Southern tish, you evah see black t.p.? Yo' all sweet lil Nefertitis but Ah's gonna' check out every burgah fo's Ah shows dis long lean pronto pup.

> They caught him in Frisco to seal his fate
> At San Quentin they jailed him one evening late
> But out on de ocean John did escape
> 'Cause someone forgot to close de golden gate

> He was long gone
> Frob Kentucky
> Long gone
> Ain't he lucky
> Long gone
> What Ah mean
> Long Gone John frob Bowling Green

Den de Prebident o' dese bigra Nigra collegiums put his ham on mah shouldah n' say, "Son, you're a credit to the riot." N'Ah says, "Fathah Prebident, yo all be mah daddy? Las' time Ah saw you, you chantin' 'Wha's de word Thundahbird', n' you rolls obah in de broken glass n' de blood pour down on de floor o' de paddy wagon n'Ah stan's dere n' Ah's weepin' alligatah big ones, daddy, yo mah daddy?"

> Iz Ah iz
> Or Iz Ah ain't
> Yo baby

N' de Prebident say, "My boy, you're not to present these stereotypes. They tear down the image we here at G.W.B. Dublanche try so hard to maintain." "Zat where Ah iz, papah?" N' de Prebident say, "I am your spiritual father, your development comes from the spirit of my loins. But I am not your real father, I am your Dean and your Doctor." "Papa Dean Doctah, yo say dis is G.W.B Duvalier hoodoo boodoo, Ah's burnin' a pin-pricked doll on yo' front lawn, sawbones. Now Ah knows it. Ah iz yo baby. Yo be mah natural, no, processed, daddy. You iz daddy bank robber become Prebident o' de bigges' nigres' collegium i' all de down home."

> Long gone frob Kentucky
> Long gone ain't he lucky
> Long gone
> What Ah mean
> Long Gone John frob Bowling Green
> Yuk yuk yuk yuk yuk yuk yuk

HE yuks off. MESHACH strolls in.

MESHACH: Two monks, Akito and Kim, both of an Oriental persuasion, were walking down a road after a recent rainfall.

Ahead of them stood a beautiful young woman. Her bare feet were dry and her dress was pressed. Before her lay a large puddle. Without asking if he might help, Akito picked her up and carried her across the water and mud. He then set her down and without a word continued on his way. Kim followed. That night the monks found shelter in a monastery. Before retiring, Kim, who had been silent since the incident on the road, spoke. "Akito, you know we monks must have nothing to do with women. Yet you took that girl in your arms and carried her several yards." Akito replied, "Kim, I left her back on that road. Are you still carrying her?"

MESHACH *goes to his judge's position as* SHADRACH *à la Porgy on his flat car*, and ABED-NEGO *enter and take theirs.*

DANIELLE *&* NEBUCHADNEZZAR *present.*

DANIELLE: All rise for Shadrach Meshach and Abed-nego.

SHADRACH (*holding a piece of paper*): Now Neb, Ah has here in mah hand a point o' disordah n' disjustice. Ah ain't comin' crawlin', no suh, you sees dat plain 'nuff. No crawlin', but wheelin' cuz Ah gots mah pride n' Ah gots mah porgy-mobile, bes' way a double ampuknee gits hisself roun'.

DANIELLE: I object to this sick joke. You are no more without legs than I am.

SHADRACH: Le's see dem fancy walkin' wheels.

DANIELLE: See all you're going to.

SHADRACH: Dat thing o' yores ain't no good unless yo' usin' dat thing. It ain't nessa ain't nessa ain't nessa ain't nessa now Nessa Neb massa' Neb on Jewlie de 8t' did you o' did you not . . .

DANIELLE: I demand the purpose of this grandstanding.

SHADRACH: Gran' standin', dis iz de point o me o my o weeo would be gran' standin' but Ah gots me de peculyah particularity o' not bein' able to do no standin' gran o' othahhow.

DANIELLE: The Judge is obfuscating.

SHADRACH: Well, wash mah mouf if Ah evah duz dis offuskatin', dis Rockefeller Center Attica Jailhouse skatin,' Gubnah,

wid yo' pinstripes down 'roun yo' ankles, Happy Deathday
Blowjob, Massa' Nelson.

DANIELLE: The Judge has eyes, hands and legs.

SHADRACH (*Shylockly*): Has not a Judge eyes . . . yeh, we heard dis
rummagin' 'bout i' de fancy Jewlie literachur fo' de ofay-
skatin' reeferences befo'. Gib me de Bible n' de historickal
records n' de res' iz garbage, dat remin's me, Neb, wha'
kind of grub dey feedin' you?

NEBUCHADNEZZAR: Garbage.

SHADRACH: Grubbage like you gibs all us folk.

MESHACH: You're getting ahead of yourself.

SHADRACH: How can Ah be ahead o' mahself when Ah is right
here?

DANIELLE: Judge Meshach, may we have your opinion?

SHADRACH: We don' wan' no pinions, we want de hot hard facks.
On Jewlie de 8t, did you or did you not . . .

MESHACH: When a tulip's two lips press another tulip's two lips.

DANIELLE: There's joy in Mudville when Shadrach's at the bat.

MESHACH: Press your point.

SHADRACH (*waving the paper*): . . . sign dis ordah pressin' me into de
service o' yo' country?

NEBUCHADNEZZAR: I already signed it.

SHADRACH: Did you or did you not?

NEBUCHADNEZZAR: I dead I did.

SHADRACH: Ah has you where Ah wants you.

ABED-NEGO: As de bishop said to de actress.

SHADRACH: Da's enuff out of character frob you dere, Pawnfish.

ABED-NEGO: Carpe diem!

NEBUCHADNEZZAR: Diem was assassinated by the Costume Intelli-
gence Agency. On that score my blood is clean.

SHADRACH: Into de service o' yore country 'gainst de midget high yellers o' Outdo China.

DANIELLE: Judge Shadrach, the name of Nebuchadnezzar on this order called you into war. If you were so against the fighting, why didn't you resist?

SHADRACH: Resist?

DANIELLE: Object? Dodge? Evade?

SHADRACH: Da's jus' like you, skirt, runnin' roun' de issue.

DANIELLE: No one's running around except you.

SHADRACH: Ah trus' de bad taste o' dat remark do not go unnoticed.

DANIELLE: Did you expect the battlefield to be another fiery furnace from which you would emerge unharmed?

SHADRACH: If Ah be put in harm's way twice, Ah gonna be harmed 'cuz when lightnin' strikes you twice, you be double dead.

DANIELLE: Yet you're alive and walking when you're not playing games.

SHADRACH: De games Ah gonna play when we iz alone gonna show whether you be into stumps.

DANIELLE: Stump the stumps.

SHADRACH: Cuz stumps iz into you.

MESHACH snaps a switchblade under SHADRACH's chin.

As Ah looks down de blade o' dis knife Ah sees mah personal Leggageddon. Twas undah such knife Ah lost de appendages appropos to de runnin' n' de jumpin'.

MESHACH removes the blade and returns to his spot.

Ah was de bigges' basketball freak de eas' side o' de Hudson. On de playgroun' 'fore dawn drivin' fo' de bunny shots, switchin' han's like some dudes switchin' blades Frazier behin' de back through de legs all two o' dem fas' breakin' top o' de key leap you jungle bunny off de rim up

fo' de tip swisshhh Dr. J. all de way red white blue b-ball
bounce hit de open man run n' shoot grab de boards
Alcindor-block Kareemin' off de iron de Big O jam n' stuff
WILLIS read Ah barely learned to Clyde yo' mah man wid
de Rolls n' de mink covah fo' de rebolbin' bed Ah was doin'
all nevah suspeck get me no Royce lil maroon Riviera style
'nuff fo' me got me through de 12f grade n' Marquette
want me! but Neb want me first so off's Ah goes marchin'
n' asteppin' goosin' n' aduckin' when BAM! landmine no
mine o' mine Ah's lucky to crawl away frob does legs
wanted me back but no use nobody gots no b-ball scholar-
ride fo' no double ampuknee.

SHADRACH has his head in his hands.

DANIELLE: Your Honor?

MESHACH: A minute please.

SHADRACH: Nono, Ah's alright. Yo all jus' wait here, Ah be right
back.

*HE wheels off. HE is wheeled back on immediately, but HE's no longer
playing the cripple. HE's before a piano and wears dark glasses. HE
plays and sings the refrain from Ray Charles' "Georgia."*

DANIELLE: The charade continues.

SHADRACH: Quiets down dere, Sapphire.

HE starts waving that piece of paper again.

Ah has here in mah hand a point o' disorder n' disjustice.
Now Neb, Ah ain't comin lookin' fo' you. Ah sees you
plain enuff cuz behin' dese black eyes . . .

HE points to his black lenses.

. . . iz mo' black eyes n' behin dose mo' black eyes.

DANIELLE: The Court knows Judge Shadrach is not blind.

SHADRACH: Who said anythin' 'bout blindness?

DANIELLE: You're posing as a blind musician, are you not?

SHADRACH: Posin', huh? Posey, be mah posey, Sapphire.

DANIELLE: That's not my name.

SHADRACH: Wha's in a name? A posey by any othah name n' Ah'd sniff you jus' de same.

SHADRACH sniffs all around HER.

Say dere, Rubah, when's de las' time . . .

MESHACH: That's enough. Move on to what's at hand.

ABED-NEGO: What Judge Shadrach thinks is at hand is something he hasn't touched for years.

SHADRACH (*to ABED-NEGO*): Who you be touchin' dese days, some little hairless poon?

ABED-NEGO: Nigger.

SHADRACH: Baiter.

ABED-NEGO: Nigger-baiter.

SHADRACH: Da's you alright.

DANIELLE: The charge?

SHADRACH: On de 9t o' Jewlie did you or did you not, Massa' Neb . . .

ABED-NEGO: I object to the pronunciation of July.

SHADRACH: I's about time. On de 9t o' Augus' did you or did you not . . .

DANIELLE: One second. Is it July or August?

SHADRACH: On de 9t o' Jewlie . . .

ABED-NEGO: July.

SHADRACH: . . . did you or did you not sign dis ordah pressin' Ruthie Begonyah into de service o' Mabel Lee Cartwright o' Tuscaloosa, Alabama?

MESHACH: Where do you find elephants with dentures?

DANIELLE: In Alabama where the tusks are loosa.

SHADRACH: Did you or did you not?

NEBUCHADNEZZAR: I die I did.

SHADRACH: Now Ruthie Begonyah performed her duties for twenty years 'til one day she was found collapsed i' de pantry. Tryin' to keep herself frob fallin' she grabbed onto de nearest thing.

ABED-NEGO: What was that thing?

SHADRACH: An old cocoa jar it was.

ABED-NEGO: Now Missa's lyin' i' de coco groun's.

SHADRACH: Ah notices when de convenience iz wid de Justice fo' de full-scale interrupshun o' de cause o' true Justice . . .

ABED-NEGO gives HIM the Bronz, of course I mean Bronx, cheer.

De chil' molestah is evrywhere aboundin'.

ABED-NEGO: Prove it, El Dorko.

SHADRACH: You talks mo' dan you thinks. De interrupshun Ah duzn't has to proob. De molestation in time will speak fo' itsellfs.

NEBUCHADNEZZAR: Did I or did I not? Yes!

SHADRACH: At de ebent o' de fallin' o' Ruthie Begonyah aforesaid Ruthie was carryin' chile. Dat chile was Sapphire P. Divine.

NEBUCHADNEZZAR: Father Divine of Philadelphia.

SHADRACH: He was de fathah o.k. frob de city of brotherly HAH! n' blubbery Rizzo.

DANIELLE: Your Honor, I would not be allowed to make topical references.

SHADRACH: Too bed fo' you, step-sister.

DANIELLE: Judge Meshach?

MESHACH: We have practically everything on the menu.

DANIELLE: I see. Could you bring me a clean one?

MESHACH: Shadrach will refrain from topical therefore extraneous references.

SHADRACH: Say, where duz you get off tellin' me wha's extranus?

MESHACH: Where duz you get off tellin' me what's extranus?

SHADRACH: Sapphire P. Divine was an incubatah doll dere's de apprentice-baitah n' de journeyman baitah n' de incubatah. She too fell into de service o' de Cartwright family dis time undah de titelage o' Margo Sue Cartwright o' Talahatchet, Loseiana. Habin' hatchied frob de incubatah, Sapphire was a chick o' de uncommonest desire fo' poppin' out many a chillun but alack n' alas fo' dis po' brown lass, she had de fertility mange.

DANIELLE: The point, the point.

SHADRACH: Ah promises you, stick to de point n' de point will stick you.

ABED-NEGO: What is the point?

SHADRACH: Gangin' on me, hey?

MESHACH: Bang! What's the charge?

SHADRACH: Hol' back or Ah's callin' de NAAJB 'n if you doesn't know what JB stan's fo' you knows knowthing.

ABED-NEGO: 'Bout Jungle Bunnies.

SHADRACH: We knows mo' dan you thinks 'bout you n' de adolescent one, 'n da's much mo' dan you thinks.

NEBUCHADNEZZAR: Sapphire P. Divine bore one child. During early pregnancy she contracted disease from Robert Lee Cartwright. The circumstances are unclear.

SHADRACH: Rape!

NEBUCHADNEZZAR: The child, called Ray Wonder, was born blind.

SHADRACH: Did you or did you not on Jewlie de 9t sign dis ordah pressin' Ruthie Begonyah into de service o' Mabel Lee Cartwright dereby direckly leadin' to de blindness o' me Ray Wonder?

DANIELLE: He has already answered the question. Will the Justice proceed?

SHADRACH (*going off stage and returning in a wheel chair*): Mah pleasure.

ABED-NEGO (*reading*):
> "I saw, and behold a tree in the midst of the earth.
> The tree was grown and had become strong
> And the height reached unto heaven
> And the sight to the end of all the earth
> The leaves were fair and the fruit much
> The beasts of the field had shadow under it
> And all flesh was fed by it."

NEBUCHADNEZZAR: My dream!

SHADRACH: So it's time, is it?

MESHACH: Time.

SHADRACH: "A holy one came down from heaven. He cried aloud and said thus: Hew down the tree and cut off its branches, shake off its leaves and scatter its fruit; let the beasts get away from under it and the fowls from its branches so that all the living may know that the Lord God Most High rules in the kingdom of men."

DANIELLE: "The tree that you saw whose height reached unto heaven, it is you, o King, that has grown and become strong, for your greatness reaches to heaven and your dominion to the end of the earth."

SHADRACH (*again waving the paper*): I has here in mah hand a point o' disordah n' disjustice. Now, Massa' Neb, is it true you is de owner n' de operator o' Hun City?

NEBUCHADNEZZAR: Hun City? I did own Sun City and Fun City.

SHADRACH: Fun City Ah calls Gun City. Saturday night's a very special night 'specially when you Massa' Neb iz de bigges' manufacturah. No, dis iz Hun H-U-N City.

NEBUCHADNEZZAR: I've never heard of it.

SHADRACH: You nevah heard o' de Duke County Rehabilitation n' Maintenance Center fo' de Aged n' Infirm?

NEBUCHADNEZZAR: Why, yes.

SHADRACH: N' will you still tell me you nevah heard o' Hun City?

NEBUCHADNEZZAR: To the better of my recollection, perhaps I have heard of it.

SHADRACH: Iz you aware dat yo' name iz on de deed fo' de Duke County Rehabilitation n' Maintenance Center fo' de Aged n' Infirm?

NEBUCHADNEZZAR: Yes, I am aware.

SHADRACH: Den, iz you also aware dat de head honcho, de man who administrates de Center you own is one S.S. Reichmann de T'ird, known to dose who dare raise dere breaths as Attila de Hun?

NEBUCHADNEZZAR: Reichmann III, yes.

SHADRACH: N' dat he hisself iz proud o' de name n' refers to de center as Hun City?

NEBUCHADNEZZAR: No, I didn't.

DANIELLE: He has answered the question.

NEBUCHADNEZZAR: I no longer own it, I gave it up.

SHADRACH: Iz you aware dat on Jewlie de 10t a woman confined to a wheelchair was beaten wid de ibory cane o' dis Reichmann?

NEBUCHADNEZZAR: I believe I did hear something about it.

SHADRACH: All becuz an attendant forgot to apply de brake.

NEBUCHADNEZZAR: As I heard it the wheel chair rammed into the head administrator.

SHADRACH: Obah de tip o' his boot iz de eyewitness account. What did you do about dis matter?

NEBUCHADNEZZAR: I considered firing him.

SHADRACH: You considered deprivin' yo'self o' de best money-rakah dis side o' Gun City, de man so skillful at skimmin' off de top dat de National Milk Producers of which you was head awarded S. S. de Croix o' de creme de la Creme?

NEBUCHADNEZZAR: Those are wild accusations.

SHADRACH: Dey was wild profits.

DANIELLE: "O King, it is the decree of the Most High that thou shall be driven from men and thy dwelling shall be with the beasts of the field and thou shalt be made to eat grass as oxen and shall be wet with the dew of heaven and seven times shall pass over thee til thou know that the Most High ruleth in the Kingdom of Men and giveth it to whomsoever He will. Wherefore, let my counsel be acceptable unto thee and break off thy sins by righteousness and thine iniquities by showing mercy to the poor if there may be a lengthening of thy tranquillity."

SHADRACH: Break off thy sins by righteousness, show mercy to the poor. Massa' Neb, did you clean up Hun City?

NEBUCHADNEZZAR: I tried.

SHADRACH: Gun City?

NEBUCHADNEZZAR. Yes.

SHADRACH: Sun City?

NEBUCHADNEZZAR: A little.

SHADRACH: Yo' poppy fields?

NEBUCHADNEZZAR: Which ones?

SHADRACH: Yo' munitions plants?

NEBUCHADNEZZAR: I don't recollect.

SHADRACH: To de best. Yo' pharmaceutical monopolies?

NEBUCHADNEZZAR: You go too fast.

DANIELLE: Stop!

SHADRACH: Yo' speed factories?

NEBUCHADNEZZAR: Pills?

SHADRACH: Yo' preservative laboratories doin' research on de elimination o' de misfits, de marginal misfits n' anybody anywhere doin' anythin' you don' like or considahs a threat to what you hold profane. Profanity, Massa' Neb, you iz de one who puts polysorbate 80 in my Velveeta n' de BHA in mah Mazola n' knows it's gonna kill me befo' Ah learns to pronounce mono-polydiglycerides. You iz de god o' Triage, baby, but it's endin' here n' now.

NEBUCHADNEZZAR: My poppies!

SHADRACH (*HE's off somewhere*): Poppy? You mah Pops?

MESHACH: "All this came upon the King Nebuchadnezzar."

> SHADRACH *snaps out of it.*

SHADRACH: Justice Abed-nego, will you do the honors?

ABED-NEGO (*reading*): "At the end of twelve months he was walking in the royal palace of Babylon. The King spake and said . . . "

NEBUCHADNEZZAR: Is this not great Babylon which I have built for the royal dwelling place by the might of my power and the glory of my majesty?

ABED-NEGO: "While the word was in the King's mouth, there fell a voice from heaven saying, 'The kingdom is departed from thee.' The same hour was the thing fulfilled upon Nebuchadnezzar and he was driven from men and did eat grass as oxen and his body was wet with the dew of heaven 'til his hair was grown like eagle's feathers and his nails like birds claws."

> *Lights down on all except* NEBUCHADNEZZAR.

NEBUCHADNEZZAR: I am running on a foot track and carrying a basket in my right hand. The basket is filled with goods and on top is a small animal I can't identify. The animal keeps falling off. I often manage to catch it before it falls to the ground and still maintain my pace. When I am not successful, I stop and pick it up. It is then I am aware of a woman running with me. She asks me questions. I can't answer them. "Why are you running like an elephant from the plum trees?" I start running again and for a full revolution the animal does not fall off and the woman does not make herself known. Then it begins again.

STOP.

I unexpectedly meet a woman I have not seen for a year. I have lusted after her since we met, but nothing has come of it. Tonight there will be a climax, sexual or otherwise. We are in a cafe at a table with many people. A brute and a boor sits across and tries to monopolize her. She is neither interested in him nor me but another man next to her. I announce that I am going. She says, "Go." I do not. We are on the floor of her apartment. I am over her but not on top of her. The rug must be coarse on her back for it is rough on my hands as I continue to suspend myself above her. She twirls veils in front of me teasing me with glimpses of her body. I keep my distance.

DANIELLE enters his light.

DANIELLE: You have trouble steering an auto at a curve. A woman will be hit. You can't run on a track without your progress halted. You try to stop; you try to go. You persist in thinking there's a difference. Put the animal down. Leave the basket. It will no doubt eat the contents and be delighted without you. Go on your way. If the woman makes herself known, tell her to run the other way for one revolution. You continue on your way also for one revolution. When you have both returned to the same point, think if there's anything to be said for coming and going

She twirls veils in front of her body teasing you with glimpses and you keep your distance. But there is no distance, you deceive yourself. You have possessed her often and deeply enough. Did you not say you lusted after her? Give it up, pack it in. When you let go the wheel, the car stops.

Lights off THEM and up on SHADRACH MESHACH & ABED-NEGO, unbound, ungagged relaxing in the midst of the fiery furnace. The FOURTH MAN is among THEM.

JUDGES: Praise the Lord!

SHADRACH: N' pass de Remy Martin.

The FOURTH MAN passes HIM the Remy Martin.

Yassuh, Richie de Itch, las' time Ah saw you you was tryin' to git me to come in on dat drycleanin' stick-up.

FOURTH MAN: "No, m'man, Ah's clean," you said.

SHADRACH: So's you went ahead n' hit de place widout me.

FOURTH MAN: Den Ah took me de cash back to mah pad n' went out fo' some celebration. When Ah got back, some nigger'd done rifled all dat bread.

SHADRACH: Cain't nevah 'magine who dat nigger was.

HE passes the bottle to ABED-NEGO.

ABED-NEGO: I don't remember you from the Legion.

FOURTH MAN: You're not trying hard enough.

ABED-NEGO: They disbarred me, you know.

FOURTH MAN: Reinstatement is possible.

ABED-NEGO: My crime, misdemeanor, was a misunderstanding.

FOURTH MAN: No it wasn't, and if you admit it you will be forgiven.

ABED-NEGO passes the bottle to MESHACH.

MESHACH: I would be better off in chains. Freedom does not become me.

FOURTH MAN: You are not free.

MESHACH: What am I?

FOURTH MAN: Released.

SHADRACH begins the last chorus of Ray Charles' "Unchain my heart." MESHACH and ABED-NEGO back HIM up as the fiery furnace becomes the Courtroom. The FOURTH MAN has disappeared as the JUDGES take their positions.

DANIELLE: Nebuchadnezzar has been charged with causing crippling, blinding and cruelty for maximum financial profit. By his own admission he has at least contributed to those crimes. He seems to deserve punishment, but who among you will mete it out . . .

SHADRACH: Ah.

DANIELLE: . . . when the Lord God on High saw fit to raise Nebuchadnezzar to his former glory. Would you in the name of Justice pretend to do what the Lord would not? Are you saying the Lord is unjust?

SHADRACH: It was not the Lord God on High who was maimed n' blinded n' beaten wid an ibory cane!

MESHACH (*to* NEBUCHADNEZZAR): Do you have anything to say before I ask the question?

NEBUCHADNEZZAR remains silent.

Are you guilty or not?

NEBUCHADNEZZAR produces his flute and blows two identical notes.

Not.

End ACT TWO.

ACT THREE

Light on ABED-NEGO.

ABED-NEGO: The train enters the station. We are home from Miami. The mother greets us. Eva introduces me to the mother who I've known for years though not well. "Bobka was very good to us and only naughty once," she says as she moves on with her small companion. The mother does not ask me for an explanation. I act as if none is needed. At lunch the little girl with the flat-backed tomato head is vigorous in her praise of Miami. I remind her we stayed in a motel across the street from which was a trailer camp filled with retired circus dwarves. She does not laugh. She has heard the line before and now ignores it. After lunch the mother invites me to stay for dinner. Eva hears, but does not respond. She shows her mother snapshots we've taken at Disneyland, Dolphin Park, Sturgeon Square, Pompano Isthmus, God, your Honor, I don't remember all the spots. "Here's a picture of our train and this is the top bunk where Bobka slept." I again act as if no explanation is needed. My naughtiness goes unmentioned. Dinner, then I am asked to stay the night. The mother, claiming headache, retires. Eva's companion is gone. The two of us remain before the fire. She says, "Naughty." We hear pounding on the floor above. I rush to the landing and open the door. The mother is behind it in a sleepwalk. She moves down the hall. I follow her, turn into the room assigned to me, go to my knees and say what I recall from the rosary.

ABED-NEGO *leaves the light.* SHADRACH *enters.*

SHADRACH: So's de aldermanic association o' greatah Jekyll n' Hyde Park comes to me n' sayz "Rastus, how's you like to run 'gainst de Mayah o' dis burg Richard J. Monthly?" N' Ah sayz, "Shit on a Good Humah stick, man, Ah's de feline to takes him on." So's Ah starts campaignin' on de weed roots platform. Populist, Ah iz n' Populist Ah remains. *Pop*ulist Daddy-u-list, u dig? Who mah daddy no matter, who Richard J. Monthly's daddy nobody care Ah's walkin' along one night n' all dese limolemonsines dey's parked double quadruple roun' de Courthouse seems Richard J.'s son he habin' a biggesh blast 'cuz he's marryin' de daughtah o' Sam de Futznutz Gianconman membah extra-ordinaire o' de mamafias n' de mamaCIAs so Ah gets me mah camera snappin' away a' dese illegal parked Sisillyan cherryots when dis Policeman biggesh black mutha dude he got so many chins Ah say, "Chin yo'self" n' he says "Which one?" den he bust me 'cross de lens n' de greasies' shiny-suited Evil-atra evah he bust me a good one den jump in his Monte Carlo and gun down de Lake Shore Drive wid police sirens escortin' him home to de onyx bathtubs he numbahs frob de numbahs rackets tennis elbow anyone dat cop broke both mah funny bones thought Ah'd die laughin now back in de South Side gin mills Ah gets me some tv coverage n' duz de hungah strike n' de vegetarian bit n' Ah gets all o' two hunnerd votes what wid Richard J. Monthly's cronies handin' out de two dollar bills n' de diseased chickens at ebry pollin' place. What could Ah gib de votah 'sides de uncertain heritage of de

    Iz Ah iz
    Or iz Ah ain't
    Yo' baby

SHADRACH *leaves the light.* MESHACH *enters.*

MESHACH: Some people work; others tell stories. Still others do both, but that's a different matter. Workers call story-tellers shirkers. The story-tellers think the workers fools, though they don't think this aloud for the workers have the strength to destroy them, though more likely they kill themselves. If pressed, the word-people envy workers their activity, so much that word people have taken to work, not that they like it much, but want to speak about it with some authority. In turn, workers—policemen, fire-men and soon sanitationmen—now write about their work for they think making words, and perhaps it is so, is easier than doing work. Thus, the distinction between worker and worder becomes blurred. A man calling him-self poet met a woman calling herself worker at a demon-stration for more food at lower costs. When some of their demands had been met, the two shared a meal. At the end of the food, he broke his pen and she threw down her hammer. Looking for the rest of the answer, they then built a fire with his notes and made love in the bed she had built. As they spoke to each other in loving ways, he remembered driving the nails and she the oaths she had cried.

MESHACH *leaves the light. We are now in the courtroom.*

DANIELLE: All rise for Justices Shadrach Meshach and Abed-nego.

SHADRACH, MESHACH & ABED-NEGO *take their places.* NEBUCHADNEZZAR *and* DANIELLE *on their feet.*

DANIELLE: Your Honors, I move for a mis-trial.

ABED-NEGO: On what grounds?

DANIELLE: The only charges have proved after the fact. Must I repeat that Nebuchadnezzar has been forgiven by the Almighty? Sons of men have dubious right to consider punishment of other sons of men.

ABED-NEGO (*an exclamation*): Jesus!

SHADRACH: Sunny beaches, son o' man, da's who Ah iz.

ABED-NEGO: If you are right, Ms. Counsel, then the Almighty will punish the would-be punishers. You will have nothing to say.

DANIELLE: I will have had my say.

ABED-NEGO: Two charges have been brought against this man; the third is this:

ALL are silent as a hand appears and writes the words "Mene Mene Tekel Upharsin."

DANIELLE: Mene Mene Tekel Upharsin.

SHADRACH: Meanie meanie tickle oopboopbeedoop.

SHADRACH gets the hiccoughs. In front of HIM DANIELLE forms the Cross with her arms.

You got da wrrrong vampire!

HE stops hiccoughing.

NEBUCHADNEZZAR: Now if thou canst read the writing and make known to me the interpretation thereof, thou shalt be clothed with purple and have a chain of gold about thy neck and shalt be the third ruler in the Kingdom.

DANIELLE: Let thy gifts be to thyself and give thy rewards to another. Nevertheless I will read the writing unto the King and make known to him the interpretation. Mene: God hath numbered thy kingdom and brought it to an end.

MESHACH: What do you know about classical music?

DANIELLE: There was a man known for his simultaneous hauteur and generosity.

MESHACH: WHAT DO YOU KNOW ABOUT CLASSICAL MUSIC?

DANIELLE: My great-uncle Casimir used to tickle Galla-Curci.

MESHACH & DANIELLE (*under the chin of ABED-NEGO*): Curci Curci Curci!

DANIELLE: There was a man known for his simultaneous hauteur and generosity.

MESHACH: Silence.

DANIELLE: Supplicants waited for weeks for an audience. When finally they gained entrance the man refused to look at them and told them to get out of his sight.

MESHACH: Sores for sightless eyes.

DANIELLE: As they left the castle, his servants gave them more than they had come for.

MESHACH: Who understands generosity?

DANIELLE: Your Honor, the third charge.

MESHACH: Ms. Danielle, may I call you such?

DANIELLE does not answer.

Now, Ms. Such, is it true? Is it false?

DANIELLE: Everything.

MESHACH: That you are a prophet that you are a prophet true or false?

DANIELLE: True *and* false.

NEBUCHADNEZZAR: God hath numbered my kingdom and brought it to an end.

DANIELLE: Tekel: thou art weighed in the balances.

MESHACH: Counsel shall answer only what is asked.

DANIELLE: Hauteur and generosity. One masks the other.

MESHACH: Cease.

DANIELLE: If one is only generous, one is thought a fool.

MESHACH: Who cares what *one* thinks? Desist!

DANIELLE: If one is only haughty, one is despised.

MESHACH: Who cares if one is despised? If one is haughty and generous one is a despised fool.

DANIELLE: Is it true I am a false prophet?

MESHACH: Is it false?

DANIELLE: I am not strictly speaking a prophet.

MESHACH: Strictly speaking, spare the rod and spoil the honey-dew.

SHADRACH (*singing to "Do do that Voodoo"*): Honey do do that voodoo that pin pricks so well.

MESHACH: As the actress said to the bishop.

DANIELLE: I interpret, I do not prophesy.

MESHACH: I have you where I want you.

SHADRACH: As the . . . oh, forget it.

NEBUCHADNEZZAR (*angrily*): Who is on trial? I want the third charge of the Bible Brigade and if you don't give it to me I might as well just leave.

ABED-NEGO: The court considers everything you say and then some.

NEBUCHADNEZZAR: And then some what? I ask you, is your wife better? You say, than what?

MESHACH: Quiet!

NEBUCHADNEZZAR: I WANT MY OWN JOKE!

MESHACH: At the end of the day we'll give you the leftovers.

>   *To* DANIELLE.

>   Is it not so you have dreams which you believe forecast the future?

DANIELLE: Forecast? Weather?

MESHACH: Whether or not, what is your answer?

DANIELLE: I wish we didn't have any.

MESHACH: Weather?

DANIELLE: I have no dreams. Others have them. I interpret them, I am dreamless.

MESHACH: Then what is it you have? Visions? Jeanne D'Arc?

DANIELLE: Obfuscation. We demand the third charge.

MESHACH: We?

NEBUCHADNEZZAR: We! Remember *we*?

SHADRACH: Shush on you, bucky boo, or we gonna' strangle you wid de bedsheet frub de Klan!

MESHACH: Seizures? Fits? Are you subject to?

DANIELLE: Subject *and* object: My order . . .

MESHACH: Disorder?

DANIELLE: Has nothing to do . . .

MESHACH: With everything.

DANIELLE: Is true and false.

MESHACH: You lay on the ground.

DANIELLE: And was ill.

MESHACH: And did not know . . .

DANIELLE: What anything meant.

MESHACH: Though it had been revealed.

DANIELLE: Something.

MESHACH: Upharsin.

DANIELLE: Mene Mene Tekel Upharsin.

> *As* MESHACH *proceeds,* SHADRACH *goes into the lead number of The Temptin' Temptations album.*

MESHACH: We offer you now while they last—stones, large stones. A bright young lassie would turn these jobbies into a truckful of bread. Throw yourself down on the mercy of the Court, sweetlungs, and we'll pick you up, minister to you, angel neck, why are you waiting do not hesitate to be the first on your block all this and there's more where this comes from the knees darling the knees bend thou art and to bend thou shalt return genuflect and kiss my flour sack my ashes and tan all the kingdoms of the world!

> MESHACH, SHADRACH, ABED-NEGO *and* NEBUCHADNEZZAR *go into an all-out blast of the same Temptations' number. At its end . . .*

DANIELLE: Get behind me, Temptations. God hath numbered thy kingdom and brought it to an end; thou art weighed in the balances and found wanting; thy kingdom is divided.

MESHACH: As I was saying, two charges have been brought against this man; the third is this:

HE looks about. Silence. His gaze rests on DANIELLE.

MESHACH: Counsel, do you know the third charge?

DANIELLE: It was held from me.

MESHACH: How did you know the others?

DANIELLE: They came to me, that is, I was handed the charges, typed, as part of the Court's business.

MESHACH: Typed? In what way?

DANIELLE: Without mistake.

MESHACH: Without mistake. And the third charge?

DANIELLE: It did not come, that is, I was not handed the third charge.

MESHACH: Typed.

DANIELLE: Or at all.

MESHACH: Could it be . . .

DANIELLE: Could it be what?

MESHACH: Do you know what I was going to say?

DANIELLE: No.

MESHACH: You cannot foresee?

DANIELLE: I do not foresee in the sense of prophecy. Only in the sense of interpretation. I am presented with, signs come to me, I am able to grasp the meaning of the signs and by this I . . .

MESHACH: Tell the future.

DANIELLE: I do not tell the future how to be, I simply expose what the signs reveal to me.

MESHACH: Forehear foresee forespeak.

DANIELLE: Dreamless.

MESHACH: That is next. You are so involved in the fantasy and dream life of others, including the Lord God on High I presume, that you have no fantasies, you have no dreams yourself.

DANIELLE: My clients, if you will, do that for me. But I am other things besides a repository. In this Courtroom I am foremost a judicial animal.

MESHACH: Judicious?

DANIELLE: You heard me.

MESHACH: The third charge against the King is that he threw you into the den of lions.

"Then this Counsel was distinguished above all and the King thought to set Counsel over the whole realm. Those jealous sought occasion against Counsel but could find no fault. Then said those jealous, "We shall not find any occasion against her, except concerning the law of her God." Then they went to the King and said, "Whosoever shall ask a petition of any god or man for thirty days, save of thee, o King, she shall be cast into the den of lions. Now, o King, establish the interdict and sign the writing. Wherefore the King did so. And when Counsel knew that the writing was signed, she went into her house where the windows were open toward Jerusalem."

DANIELLE: And I kneeled upon my knees three times a day and prayed and gave thanks before my God, as I did aforetime.

MESHACH: "Then those jealous assembled together and found Counsel making petition and supplication before her God. They went to the King and said 'That child of the captivity of Judah maketh petition three times a day.'"

NEBUCHADNEZZAR: Then the King when he heard these words was sore displeased and set his heart on Counsel to deliver her and he labored until dusk. But the jealous demanded that he keep his word.

MESHACH: "Then the King commanded and they brought Counsel and cast her into the den of lions."

NEBUCHADNEZZAR: Thy God whom thou servest continually will deliver thee.

MESHACH: "And a stone was brought and laid upon the mouth of the den; and the King sealed it with his own signet and with the signets of his lords that nothing might be changed."

NEBUCHADNEZZAR: Then I went to my palace and passed the night fasting as all sleep fled from me.

MESHACH: "Then the King arose very early in the morning and went in haste unto the den of lions. And when he came near he cried with a lamentable voice."

NEBUCHADNEZZAR: O servant of the living God, is thy God, whom thou servest continually, able to deliver thee from the lions?

DANIELLE: My God hath sent his Angel and hath shut the lions' mouths.

SHADRACH: Well, shut ma mouf.

DANIELLE: And they have not hurt me for innocence was found in me.

SHADRACH: Da's not all dat was found in ya.

MESHACH snaps the switchblade.

De Saturday night special gibs way to de Sunday mornin' draw n' quarter back.

MESHACH unsnaps the switchblade.

DANIELLE: And also before thee, o King, have I done no hurt.

MESHACH: "Then was the King exceedingly glad and Counsel was taken up out of the den and no manner of hurt was found because she had trusted in God."

NEBUCHADNEZZAR: And the King commanded.

DANIELLE (*dispassionately*): And they brought those men who had accused me and they cast them into the den of lions, them, their children and their wives; and the lions had the mastery of them and brake all their bones in pieces before they came to the bottom of the den.

MESHACH: Where were you when the lions "had the mastery of them"?

DANIELLE: Where were we, o King?

NEBUCHADNEZZAR. Above, looking down.

MESHACH: Into the den?

SHADRACH: Mutha.

DANIELLE: Them, their children and their wives.

MESHACH: Do you have nightmares?

DANIELLE: I am dreamless.

MESHACH: Entirely?

DANIELLE: Completely.

MESHACH: Snap.

DANIELLE: And the lions had the mastery.

MESHACH: Entirely?

DANIELLE: Absolutely.

MESHACH: Crackle.

DANIELLE: A mouse in the mouth of a cat.

MESHACH: Tail wriggling.

> *Simultaneously* MESHACH & DANIELLE *make the noise of a cat sucking in a mouse tail.*
>
> A child's foot—
>
> MESHACH & DANIELLE *make the same noise.*
>
> The last of the child, the child's toe—
>
> *Same noise.*
>
> The last of Danielle, Danielle's soul—
>
> *No noise.*
>
> Entirely?

DANIELLE: Completely.

MESHACH: Absolutely?

DANIELLE: Devastatingly dreamless.

MESHACH & DANIELLE: Dreamless.

SHADRACH: Pop.

> *Lights down on all but* NEBUCHADNEZZAR.

NEBUCHADNEZZAR: Late at night I am in a deserted area of a large city. For a moment I try to think why I am there, but I cannot take even the moment. I must concentrate on getting out. On the left are the half-standing apartment buildings of a full block. The wrecker's ball has done only half its work. I see a squad car. From the wreckage ahead stream flashlights, low voices, cursing. Two policemen, sober, are pulling two policemen, drunk, from a falling structure. To the think tank, I think, though I know I mean drunk tank. I cross the street hoping they have not seen me. Warehouses, abandoned and not, on the other side. I move quickly ahead to get out of their line of vision. They move quickly back so I cannot. Another squad car. The two drunks come to it. One gets inside behind the driver's seat. The other crosses in front of me and butts me gently in the belly with his sheep's head.

A woman I long for is having dinner in a restaurant with a man I know only by reputation. I enter with another woman but do not notice the first or her companion. The second woman points them out. The second woman and I leave by car with some others. I drive, the second woman in back. The first woman stands on an opposite corner looking in the direction we are traveling. It is raining. She is alone. As we pass I lower my window slightly and lean up to call her name through the opening. As I do, a truck passes us drowning out my voice and sending splashes against us.

DANIELLE *moves into his light.*

DANIELLE: You having trouble turning a car; you can't run without your progress halted; you can't get away from a drunken policeman butting you gently. For a moment you try to think why you are there, but you concentrate instead on getting out. But concentration is not movement. It is stillness. It wants you more than you know. You cannot get out of its line of vision. Engage it. Butt it gently with your friendly head.

A woman throws pencils at you; another twirls veils; the third is on the opposite corner. A truck passes drowning out your voice. But your window was open only slightly.

The splashes against you were nothing compared to those against her. Open the windows wide, quit this going and coming completely, give it up, pack it in. When you let go the wheel, the car stops.

NEBUCHADNEZZAR *moves out of the light.*

As for me my spirit is grieved and the visions of my head trouble me. I long to fall into a deep sleep with my face toward the ground.

Lights off DANIELLE. *Up on the fiery furnace. The* JUDGES *restless.*

SHADRACH: Can you dig it? I here now invent me a cliché. I say, dis iz where it's at. De Fiery Furnace, you got it all? Dig? Dug, duggoot.

ABED-NEGO: You got it, let's open a club.

SHADRACH: A soul spot.

ABED-NEGO: We'll call it . . .

SHADRACH & ABED-NEGO: The Fiery Furnace!

SHADRACH: Shadrach's F. F.

MESHACH: Show me the ordinary womb.

SHADRACH: Not Ah, said de big fat hen. Ah comes frob extra-ordinary innards. Shadrach's F. F. serving innard greens.

MESHACH: The fiery furnace. An ordinary womb?

ABED-NEGO: We have to call it The Fiery Furnace, not The Womb, ordinary or not.

MESHACH: But do you suppose . . .

SHADRACH: Ah wears me de supp-hose, keeps mah splendiferous legs such n' such.

ABED-NEGO: That Saturday night's the loneliest night of the week?

SHADRACH: Not at the F. F. Come on down and do the Baked Potato.

ABED-NEGO: We barbecue on the spot.

SHADRACH: On de spit. Bring an ocean of friends.

ABED-NEGO: Try our F. F. Fries.

SHADRACH: N' shake to de sounds o' Gumbo Pie n' de Chick Peas.

MESHACH: . . . that all sorts of things start in the womb? The fiery furnace, featherbedding, gerrymandering, the negative income tax? Then why not Gumbo Pie and the Chick Peas?

ABED-NEGO: Watch for our grand opening.

SHADRACH: Come on down to de F.F. 'n get yo' self de hots.

The sound of the Weather Report as we go back to the courtroom.

DANIELLE: Nebuchadnezzar has been charged with throwing me into the den of lions. False. I went in of my own accord and put my head in the mouth of each lion.

MESHACH: And having broken off your sins by righteousness your mouse tail was not swallowed. Your child's foot—

DANIELLE: Was not swallowed.

MESHACH: Your child's toe—

DANIELLE: Was not swallowed.

MESHACH: Your child's soul—

DANIELLE: My child's flat-backed tomato head, my idiot soul.

DANIELLE is a-buzz with the JUDGES' monologues that open the Acts.

DANIELLE: You carried my smell on your fingers from the North to Miami and back. You spun me around pressing my back against the coarse spread. You saw my mother in a sleep-walk, breasts bobbing. Yes, I am an idiot child, my hair is sopping, the back of my head is flat. Make me lose consciousness, make me, please.

Judge Solomon Skybumskybum, Justice Choo-Choo Justice, Judge Jud Judge n' Justice Leaner Hot Dog has all decreed i' de suupremest body o' de most exalted division o' de Prime Movah o' all Poobahs i' de sovrin' state o' Boogedy-Boogedy dat you haz no fathah but you iz *mah* baby.

The stories you tell of others are not about others. Parables usually boomerang. What does your simultaneous hauteur and generosity teach us, you who has enough silver to load thirty camels for each of us? Your method of teaching is like holding a cat's head to feed it milk. You speak of true and false. Your heart is in the wrong and right place.

MESHACH: How does Counsel plead?

DANIELLE: Counsel?

MESHACH: And they had brought those men who had accused you and cast them into the den of lions, them their children and their wives; and the lions had mastery of them and brake all their bones in pieces before they came to the bottom of the den.

Lights on DANIELLE only.

DANIELLE: Apoplexy—the breakage of a blood vessel in the brain. Apocalypse—the breakage of a blood vessel in the brain of the future/the future standing still on the Eliot point prescience pre-science revelation elation be elated it is revealed as the future lies before me/children and wives brake all their bones lions overpowered them me with my head in their mouths my whip and my chair back you devils Beatty Clyde circus three-ring Judge's three/trainer Danny/Danielle dreamless lions snoring dreaming of shepherd's pie/flies shivering about their manes pussycats brake all their bones/children and wives grieve my spirit/ trouble my head of visions in pieces/before they came to the bottom of the den/as the future lies before me it and my soul are paralyzed.

Lights on the whole Court.

MESHACH: Do you have anything to say before I ask the final question?

NEBUCHADNEZZAR is silent.

Are you guilty or not?

NEBUCHADNEZZAR hands the flute to DANIELLE. DANIELLE breaks it in two.

You have only yourselves to thank. You are found not guilty. There shall be no congratulations, no handshakes, no embraces, no celebrations and most importantly no tears.

ABED-NEGO: What? No celebration?

SHADRACH: You mean we ain't gonna gig it up?

MESHACH: What have you got to celebrate?

ABED-NEGO: The dispensation of Justice.

SHADRACH: De scales has been weighed unsealed n' delivered.

NEBUCHADNEZZAR: 'Tis time fo' puttin' on de booze bag.

SHADRACH: One mo' crack, Kingie, n' Ah's gonna arrest you fo' impeopleanatin' an Officer of de Court.

DANIELLE: N' Ah's be dressin' in some Pointer Sisters' platforms as de preparation fo' de plantin' o' mah begonyah smack on yo' rubah.

SHADRACH: Well kiss mah hide n' Zippahdeedoodah, sistah, Ah's been waitin' fo you to admit dat dat thing ain't no good 'less you usin' it.

ABED-NEGO: Yeh, Mama, what good dat thing 'less you usin' it?

MESHACH (*stripping to his nightclub finery and blowing a whistle*): Alright, everybody into the Fiery Furnace.

HE leads THEM in and THEY dance to the Weather Report.

This presentation comes to you courtesy of and is known in the trades Backstage Showbiz Variety hix nix stix plays and pix you pays us money and we gives you choice grade A number 1 high detergent 10 W 50 entertainment brought up here and now with the sound of Orange Julius and the Garbanzos Polish Power best believe it we'll Cracow your hams and suck your gelatin dry. Make us all lovely, mah honies. Verily and Amen, I say to you—this is the Sovereign State of Boogedy Boogedy.

The End.

Bicicletta

or
The Agony of the Pomegranates
in the Garden

FIRST PERFORMANCE:

December 1983, Theatre for Actors and Playwrights at Theatre
    Colonnades, New York City

Christine Neilson as Ubbidienza
Rebecca Nelson as Bicicletta
Melissa Smith as Poveretta
Brenda Thomas as Chastitata
Stephen Rowe as Stuzzicadenti

Directed by William Foeller

THE PLAYERS:

UBBIDIENZA, the Mother Superior
BICICLETTA, a nun
POVERETTA, a nun
CHASTITATA, a nun
STUZZICADENTI, a brother

THE SCENE:
A cloistered Roman Catholic convent

Rebecca Nelson as Bicicletta
(*Photograph by George and Nancy Bassarab*)

PROLOGUE

MOTHER UBBIDIENZA, in full nun's habit, SISTER BICICLETTA, barefoot and in a shift. SISTER BICICLETTA's bicycle. To the side, a man in religious robe, silhouetted, pulls a bell-rope. Twelve bells. HE exits.

UBBIDIENZA: Sister Bicicletta, fast and abstain before Mass. No food and no drink from midnight to midnight. You must receive the Eucharist on an empty stomach and a dry tongue. Now make ready to enter our Chamber of Accusation.

BICICLETTA: The Sisters of the Sacred Seed of Jesus stretch forth the long arms of their Law. When do I find out if I am a saint?

UBBIDIENZA: That is not for the here and now. This is only the beginning.

BICICLETTA: Surely this must be at least the middle.

UBBIDIENZA: Pray for strength.

BICICLETTA: How am I to consume the Host if I am dry?

UBBIDIENZA *(leaving)*: Think of lemons.

SHE has left.

BICICLETTA: I will pray for weakness.
   "How is it that you sought me? Did you not know I must be about my Father's business?"
   And they did not understand the word that He spoke to them.
   I can't remember the spelling of "school". Is it s-k-? How many "o's"?
   Holocausts of fatlings I will offer you, with burnt offerings of rams.
   Christ, I'm hungry already.

SHE sings to the tune of "Rosalie, my Rosalie."

   Rosary, my Rosary

SHE stops singing.

Aunt Wanda, why did you cut off the bottom six inches of
your closet door? Was it really to give your shoes some
air?

SHE puts her hand on the bicycle seat and goes to one knee.

Domine, non sum dignus ut intres sub tectum meum sed
tantum dic verbo et sanabitur anima mea.

SHE stands.

BICICLETTA: What's it like being with a virgin? Is there a lot of
screaming? Me? Of course not. I have never been one.

One tries to recapture one's lust for another. I mean *I* try
to recapture my first lust for *you*. You were so beautiful I
thought you had to be a fag. The two of you seemed to be
so perfect together, that woman you were with. Not perfect, but I assumed you were married *and* a fag. When I
found out you were neither, I didn't want to believe it.
Why did you ask me for that drink? Why did you touch me
with your seven hands on my body? Why did you hurt me
hurt me with someone else's key in your pocket? Always
someone else's key. How can I go to sleep without you
next to me? I can't believe you like to kiss me there. No, a
man had never come in my mouth. I am one of the most
interesting women who has ever lived and you are giving
me up. You can't hurt me because I don't want you. I mean
I don't wan CHU!

Behold my enemies are many and they hate me violently. Preserve my life and rescue me; let me not be put to
shame for I take refuge in you. Let integrity and upright-
ness preserve me, because I wait for you, O Lord.

I twirl under the clock in Grand Central. You are not
there to catch me. The train is leaving. The porter gives
me your note. Don't send me a note. Send me a person!

SHE examines her feet.

I will go to the Albergo Commendatore and there in the
basement next to the fine men being shaved I will have my
pedicure.

*SHE goes to the wash basin, dips her tooth brush in a pitcher of water,
brushes her teeth with dental powder, spits it out, wets a washrag and*

*wipes it across her teeth and tongue. SHE sits on the bicycle and lights
a Camel cigarette.*

SCENE ONE.

A cutaway confessional box. SISTER POVERETTA, *white, kneels on the
confessee's side.* SISTER CHASTITATA, *black, is the confessor. Throughout,
THEY pass and drink from a half gallon of S.S. Pierce dry sherry.*

POVERETTA: Bless me, Madre, for I have sinned. It has been only
one day since my last confession yet I have already
thought of missing my morning prayers.

CHASTITATA: Where were you when this temptation came upon
you?

POVERETTA: In the bathroom.

CHASTITATA: What were you doing in the bathroom?

POVERETTA: I was . . .

CHASTITATA: Yes?

POVERETTA: I was . . .

CHASTITATA: Yes?

POVERETTA: Going to the bathroom.

CHASTITATA: Was that all?

POVERETTA: Ah . . . yes.

CHASTITATA: Number 1 or number 2?

POVERETTA: I forget which is which.

CHASTITATA: Number 1 is . . .

POVERETTA: It was both.

CHASTITATA: When you wiped yourself . . . you did wipe yourself?

POVERETTA: Yes.

CHASTITATA: Did you touch yourself?

POVERETTA: The paper touched myself.

CHASTITATA: Not your fingers.

POVERETTA: My fingers touched the paper touching myself.

CHASTITATA: Could you feel yourself?

POVERETTA: Through the paper.

CHASTITATA: Did the paper break?

POVERETTA: Yes, I didn't mean it!

CHASTITATA: Did you use a double wad?

POVERETTA: No!

CHASTITATA: When your fingers broke through the single wad, when you touched yourself, was it then you thought of missing your morning prayers?

POVERETTA: Yes! I try I try what can I do?

CHASTITATA: You must avoid the occasion of sin. You must not go into the bathroom.

POVERETTA: Not even if I promised to use a triple wad?

CHASTITATA: You'd find a way to get so wet that your fingers would break through a whole roll!

POVERETTA: It feels good to touch myself.

CHASTITATA: It is not the goodness of Christ.

POVERETTA: Who never touched Himself?

CHASTITATA: Never.

POVERETTA: Who had others touch it for Him.

CHASTITATA: For your penance . . .

POVERETTA: When I die and go to heaven . . .

CHASTITATA: He will let you.

POVERETTA: O my God, I am heartily sorry for having offended Thee. I detest all my sins . . .

POVERETTA continues The Act of Contrition. CHASTITATA begins the "Ego Absolvo te."

SCENE TWO.

Chapel. BICICLETTA, smoking a cigarette, still dressed for bed. POVERETTA, CHASTITATA, tipsy, humming the "Dies Irae." UBBIDIENZA, swinging a smoking censor twice to the sides, twice forward. BICICLETTA lifts the censor's lid and deposits her cigarette. THEY all kneel for the rosary. The S.S. Pierce is present.

UBBIDIENZA: In the name of the Father and of the Son and of the Holy Ghost.

The SISTERS: Amen.

UBBIDIENZA: I believe in one God the Father Almighty creator of heaven and earth and in His only Son Jesus Christ . . .

SHE recites the entire Apostles' Creed, moves on to The Lord's Prayer and the three Hail Mary's which precede the body of the rosary. During this, BICICLETTA speaks.

BICICLETTA: At the beginning of my career my first husband prevented me from getting an important part in a play. He was jealous of a man who would be acting opposite me so he locked me in our one closet and refused to open the door. He then left. I screamed once and shut up. A silly young face with no talent got the part. When I became successful, I bought my husband a BMW, not the Ferrari he wanted.

Years later he called me in New York. I met him at a hotel, the Albergo Fortuna. He was wild and a little drunk. We shared a magnum of wine. At my last sip he dropped a pill into my glass. I tasted nothing. I next remember trying to dial a number I had known for years. I couldn't determine whether I should dial clockwise or counterclockwise.

You, O Lord, will keep and preserve us from this generation, while about us the wicked strut and in high places are the basest of men.

UBBIDIENZA: Let us now reflect on the Mysteries of the Rosary. The Annunciation to Mary and The Birth of Our Lord.

SHE now proceeds to say the first half of each of the ten Hail Mary's as POVERETTA and CHASTITATA answer with the second half. BICICLETTA speaks as THEY pray.

BICICLETTA: The angel of The Lord was sent to a virgin named Mary. He said, Hail full of grace, The Lord is with thee, blessed art thou among women. Behold thou shalt conceive in thy womb and bring forth a son and thou shalt call his name Jesus. But Mary said to the angel, How shall this happen since I do not know man? And the angel said to her, The Holy Spirit shall come upon thee. And Mary said, Behold the handmaiden of The Lord, be it done unto me according to Thy word.

How shall this happen to me if I *do* know man?

Arise, O God, defend your cause, remember how the fool blasphemes you day after day. Be not unmindful of the voice of your foes; the uproar of those who rebel against you is increasing.

UBBIDIENZA: The Agony in the Garden and the Crowning with Thorns.

The rosary is said as before.

BICICLETTA: The agony of the pomegranates in the garden/the favorite fruit of Jesus Christ/my soul is sad even unto death/could you not then watch this hour with me/blood sweat sweat blood watch and pray/the spirit indeed is willing but the flesh is boiling and boiling makes it weak/ behold the hour is at hand when the Son of Man will be betrayed into the hands of sinners/rise let us go he who betrays me is at hand/Aunt Wanda!/thorns through your greasy Jewboy hair/I am seeing the blood from your scalp and the oil mingle/let this cup of vinegar pass from under me/

I must stop thinking of having affairs and just have them.

UBBIDIENZA: The Crucifixion.

The rosary is said as before.

BICICLETTA: And the dumb thief said, Save yourself, Boobie, and the con man thief said, Remember me and Jesus fell for the hell game/Jesus saves Jesus saves Jesus saves/I don't care if I rush or tarry long as I got magnetic Mary/woman behold thy son and boyson thy mother and John Wayne with no awe in his voice said, Aw, it's the Son of God.

UBBIDIENZA:
And bowing His head He gave up His spirit.
The Resurrection of Our Lord.

THEY proceed with the rosary.

BICICLETTA: After three days you going to find this beat-in body rising/all those Mary's comin' lookin' fo' me/lookee here Mary/yes Mary/what's that Mary/why the rock has rolled and is not here to stay/he did never die yes he did/Mary Mary quite arbitrarily risen/now that's some mutha miracle so much for the small time/we gonna bring you to the Coliseum in Rome itself/you do dat trick we gibs you 30% of the confessional box office. The wicked are trapped by the work of their own hands/keep your hands to yourself, wicked.

Why did you hurt me hurt me with someone else's key in your pocket always someone else's key/how can I go to sleep without you next to me/to the virgin I never was/I can't believe you like to kiss me there.

UBBIDIENZA: Glory be to the Father and to the Son and to the Holy Ghost, as it was in the beginning, is now and ever shall be world without end. Amen.

The SISTERS: Amen. Alleluia. For His mercy endures forever.

BICICLETTA lights a cigarette.

POVERETTA: Smoking the strongest cigarettes and then giving up that delightful habit illustrates the ultimate message of Christ and Catholicism. "Be either hot or cold but not tepid or I shall spit you out of my mouth."

CHASTITATA: All Protestants everywhere are half-filled with luke-warm shit.

POVERETTA: A Methodist is incapable of having a vocation.

BICICLETTA: What I did on my summer vacation, by—

POVERETTA and CHASTITATA: *Vo*cation!

BICICLETTA: Don't you believe it is possible to receive a *vo*cation on a *va*cation?

CHASTITATA: Ain't we the touchy one?

BICICLETTA: Get me to a nunnery? Of course, why would I be a breeder of sinners?

UBBIDIENZA: Genuflect, Sisters. Bend the knee. To bend thou art and to bend thou shalt return.

THEY all genuflect as at the end of the Mass. POVERETTA *and* CHASTI-TATA, *the servers, flank* UBBIDIENZA, *the priest.* BICICLETTA *is apart.* POVERETTA *leaves first.* UBBIDIENZA *waits for* CHASTITATA *to cross in front of her, then follows them out.*

BICICLETTA: I was up a tree trying to be a girl scout, that is, I couldn't burn a marshmallow. I mean I wouldn't fight a girl who didn't want me to be a scout. She was bullying me, but I was quicker. I pushed her, slap against the chest. She fell back, head against a grill. She screamed and chased me. I was up a tree without no paddle, without my scab! I had lost the big scab on my elbow. No! There it was on my knee. I put it in my mouth. When it was soft, I swallowed. As it slid down, I knew God needed me. Not so much a call as a buzz. It has taken me so long to get from there, my vacation, to here. Buzz, buzz, my brother Hamlet.

SHE starts to light another cigarette, but stops.

If I want a cigarette, but wait a minute to have one, that is denying myself. I have gained actual grace. I would never give up smoking.

SHE lights her cigarette.

Think of all the grace I'd be losing.

SCENE THREE.

BICICLETTA's room. SHE's still smoking, still dressed for bed.

BICICLETTA: In third grade I put my bare legs across the aisle onto the boy's seat next to me. He touched my knees. Though stick-thin, my legs have always been the loveliest. I have told myself that every day since I first heard it.

In God, in whose promise I glory, in God I trust without fear; what can flesh do against me?

STUZZICADENTI (*off stage*): Permesso?

BICICLETTA: Avanti.

STUZZICADENTI (*entering*): I thought you might want to do the scene again.

BICICLETTA: Yes. Please give me my first line.

STUZZICADENTI: "I had my coat on I said goodbye . . ."

BICICLETTA: Of course. "I had my coat on I said goodbye to everybody twice and still I came back in so I could . . ."

STUZZICADENTI: "Could what? Certainly not talk to me. Every furry jackass in the hall has your attention but to me you don't say a word."

BICICLETTA: ". . . look at you."

STUZZICADENTI: "Look at me."

BICICLETTA: "So I could *look* at you."

STUZZICADENTI: "Now the zodiac nonsense. Strong sexual attraction but nothing in common."

BICICLETTA: "You can't hurt me."

STUZZICADENTI: "I already have."

BICICLETTA: "We haven't been married for twenty years. I have no obligations to you."

STUZZICADENTI: "Who writes your material? Change your line. I've heard it a dozen times."

BICICLETTA: "You hurt me."

STUZZICADENTI: "I can't. Remember?"

BICICLETTA: "You don't promise me love, love-making, then make a date with someone else!"

STUZZICADENTI: "You were late. You were supposed to be here. We would have made love. But you're never where you say you're going to be."

BICICLETTA: "I have no obligations to you."

STUZZICADENTI: "Fuck off."

BICICLETTA: "You."

STUZZICADENTI: "Fuck me."

BICICLETTA: "Anytime."

STUZZICADENTI: "You said you couldn't stand the thought of my being with someone else."

BICICLETTA: "All your girls! I know what you do."

STUZZICADENTI: "That you didn't think you could touch someone else."

BICICLETTA: "That I never knew I had so much skin until you touched me. I think I don't want you."

STUZZICADENTI: "Don't want me. There's this James Baldwin book. He describes a young girl's feelings as she's having sex for the first time. How can a fag get her so perfectly?"

BICICLETTA: "How do you know? Have you ever been a young girl?"

STUZZICADENTI: "No and I've never been a fag either."

BICICLETTA: "Then everything's ahead of you. You *are* a fag. I know it!"

STUZZICADENTI: "O, probably."

BICICLETTA: "Have you ever been with a virgin? What's it like? Is there a lot of screaming?"

STUZZICADENTI: "You don't know because you never were a virgin."

BICICLETTA: "You don't love me."

STUZZICADENTI: "I do, but don't make it impossible for me."

BICICLETTA: "O, look love, I want my privacy."

STUZZICADENTI: "Have it, but don't wake me in the middle of the night to tell me 'I love you so much I'm so happy with you how can I go to sleep without you?'"

BICICLETTA: "O, stop!"

STUZZICADENTI: "Yes, I know. I can't hurt you."

BICICLETTA: "You can't."

STUZZICADENTI: "Obligations."

BICICLETTA: "None."

STUZZICADENTI: "We were driving. You didn't have to say. Driving and making love. Both ways I was inside you. You said, 'Let's never do anything for each other out of obligation.' I said, 'Yes.' Then you said, 'Except to make love.' I said, 'You mean if I can't stand you or anything about you and you want to make love, I should feel obligated. Right?'"

BICICLETTA: "Yes."

STUZZICADENTI: "And do it."

BICICLETTA: "Yes."

STUZZICADENTI: "Neither of us has a veto."

BICICLETTA: "Neither."

STUZZICADENTI: "You can demand and so can I."

BICICLETTA: "Under my Grandmother's quilt."

STUZZICADENTI: "Under your Grandmother's quilt."

BICICLETTA: "Of course."

THEY are out of the scene.

STUZZICADENTI: I felt better. How about you?

BICICLETTA: It's not good.

STUZZICADENTI: Perhaps it's because you lived the scene and now you're playing it.

BICICLETTA: Did you say "lived the scene and now playing it"? Sorry. My affairs are moral, mysterious, honest, sacred. Others? Sordid. Immoral. When is the last time you had an affair?

STUZZICADENTI: Never.

BICICLETTA: What I'm trying to give up is not the affairs, though that isn't—never?

STUZZICADENTI: Yes.

BICICLETTA: It is you I should love. Perhaps if you were fat and a bit bald. I like those men with the string ties and the insurance forms. But do you mean literally?

STUZZICADENTI: I think so.

BICICLETTA: Ah, you're wavering. The exercise doesn't count, of course.

STUZZICADENTI: I'm in shape.

BICICLETTA: Doing it to keep the muscles toned, yes. Large drunken men are best for that. Just getting out from under them is like two hours in a gym.

STUZZICADENTI: Every morning I jump rope.

BICICLETTA: The bell rope, is it? I've heard you.

STUZZICADENTI: If you jump with me, you'll stop thinking about having affairs.

BICICLETTA: That's an intriguing line.

STUZZICADENTI: I'm serious and I'm not trying to be seductive.

BICICLETTA: Love, I know you are serious and I know you don't fuck around and maybe you did when you were sixteen in a rowboat with somebody's sister, but I could no more jump rope than I could walk a tight rope.

STUZZICADENTI: Christ said, He who lusts after another man's wife has already committed adultery in his heart.

BICICLETTA: With my index finger he wiped up the last drop of sperm and put it on my tongue.

STUZZICADENTI: Onan?

BICICLETTA: O no, I have never had an affair. Can I fuck everybody, can I have fucked everybody, have three husbands,
have had three, no affairs and still give myself to God?

STUZZICADENTI: To God who gives joy to my youth.

BICICLETTA: Or at least to my bicycle?

> *BICICLETTA begins to dress.* STUZZICADENTI *assists HER.*

And there was a woman who for twelve years had had a
hemorrhage and had suffered much at the hands of several physicians and had spent all that she had and found
no benefit but rather grew worse. Hearing about Jesus,
she came up behind Him in the crowd and touched His
cloak. For she said, "If I touch but His cloak, I shall be
saved." And at once the flow of her blood was dried up and
she felt in her body that she was healed of her affliction.

STUZZICADENTI: And Jesus perceiving in Himself that power had
gone forth from Him turned to the crowd and said, "Who
touched my cloak?" And His disciples said to Him, "Thou
seest the crowd pressing upon Thee and dost Thou say
'Who touched me?'"

BICICLETTA: But the woman fearing and trembling, knowing what
had happened within her, came and fell down and told
Him the truth.

STUZZICADENTI: And He said to her, "Daughter thy faith has saved
thee. Go in peace and be thou healed in thy affliction."

BICICLETTA: I have a kind of peace, but I am not healed.

> *BICICLETTA is dressed.*

SCENE FOUR.

> *UBBIDIENZA, POVERETTA and CHASTITATA at the altar table-judge's bench.*
> *BICICLETTA.*

BICICLETTA: I am Bicicletta, a Sister of the Sacred Seed of Jesus, at
whose name every head shall bow.

SHE bows her head. SHE lifts her head.

I give myself to the Savior and to his mother the Blessed Virgin who crushed the serpent with her heel.

SHE waits.

UBBIDIENZA: As you know, Sister, for us to simulate the sound of the Blessed Virgin crushing the head of the serpent is optional.

BICICLETTA: I want to hear it.

UBBIDIENZA: Imagine it.

Silence.

Sister? Imagine it faster. You were an actress, use your sense memory and no going off. Instant recall. The head of the serpent crushed.

POVERETTA: Imagine you are running over him with your bicycle.

BICICLETTA: To our founding saint, Maria Maddalena, the Sacred Vessel, whose courageous martyrdom prevented the Body of Our Lord Jesus Christ from being defiled.

SHE rattles this off.

And other Persons of the Blessed Trinity, Father and Holy Ghost, the rest of the saints known and unknown, the faithful everywhere especially our Pope Tomato Pie XII, Cardinal What's-his-name.

UBBIDIENZA: Name him.

BICICLETTA: Octaloonacci, our Bishop Pizzicatta, our Pastor Kushinski . . .

UBBIDIENZA: Dead.

BICICLETTA: And all the religious and lay who shake up this vale of tears.

THE OTHERS: Amen.

UBBIDIENZA: Poveretta, conduct the first charge of the Miracle Brigade.

POVERETTA: Are you aware, Sister, that a woman in Athens, Massachusetts . . .

BICICLETTA: Lil' Sof' Lil'.

POVERETTA: . . . at the age of 82 seems to have been cured of cancer of the face and credits you with the "miracle"?

BICICLETTA: Yes.

POVERETTA: The speculation is about your *purported* supernatural powers. The fact is the people of Athens believe Lil' when she tells them that the Mad Jingler biked several hundred miles to stand in the town square and sing:

POVERETTA and CHASTITATA sing to "Ain't She Sweet":

> Ain't it neat, all the gurus love my feet
> But it's Yogi Boopie Yogi Boopie who can't be beat
> Just cast an eye in his direction
> O me o my what an erection

UBBIDIENZA: Cut!

THEY do.

BICICLETTA: I sang nothing of the sort.

POVERETTA: Why then has it become a hit song?
Bicicletta, do you claim this cancer cure as your miracle?

BICICLETTA: How am I supposed to know?

POVERETTA: Did God speak to you?

BICICLETTA: I spoke to Him. "Deign, O Lord, to rescue me. Let them who desire my ruin be turned back."

POVERETTA: Don't threaten me.

BICICLETTA: Just keeping the memory in practice. May I smoke?

POVERETTA: No.

UBBIDIENZA: Yes.

BICICLETTA: It's got to be unanimous. Forget it.

POVERETTA: Yes.

BICICLETTA: Trying to prevent me from gaining actual grace?

POVERETTA: Why not? There will be more left over for me.

BICICLETTA: It is not as if there is only so much. For example, when I say that orgasm is the ultimate manifestation of Actual Grace . . .

CHASTITATA: You done said two mouthfuls.

BICICLETTA: I mean only when one considers God's pleasure first.

POVERETTA: Mother, do I have to be lectured, I who won the all-St. Tarcissus catechetical litany bee?

UBBIDIENZA: This is not a litany bee. No one is pitting your holiness against another's. Make your next point.

POVERETTA: It is said by Lily Benevenuto, Lil' Sof' Lil', and believed by the people of Athens that you bicycled 900 miles to sing in the town square. You do admit you sang something.

BICICLETTA: Sure.

POVERETTA: Sure what?

BICICLETTA: Sure I sang something.

POVERETTA: How long were you gone?

BICICLETTA: Six days.

POVERETTA: How is it possible?

BICICLETTA: Twenty miles per hour twenty-four hours 480 miles. Two days with a sixty-mile time-out with Lil', and peeing at vegetable road stands.

POVERETTA: It was January. Where did you find an open vegetable stand?

BICICLETTA: I'd never pee at an *open* stand.

POVERETTA: Do you expect us to believe that you squatted at closed vegetable stands in January sometime during the sixty-mile time-out for such activity and lunch?

BICICLETTA: Of course I squatted. What do you think, I let it run down my legs? Although there is a way, if you're very careful, and *when* are you going to ask me what I did with the other four days?

POVERETTA: Did it have something to do with a man?

BICICLETTA: It is difficult for me to walk my bicycle across the street without having a man in my hand or my brain. It was in Ohio. He hailed me over, strapped my bicycle to his camper and off we went.

POVERETTA: Where?

BICICLETTA: The next state.

POVERETTA: Pennsylvania?

BICICLETTA: In the tunnels?

POVERETTA: Did he get into the habit?

BICICLETTA: In the tunnels?

POVERETTA: Anywhere.

BICICLETTA: He said *it* was his first nun.

POVERETTA: *It?*

BICICLETTA: I!

POVERETTA: After you sang, you asked to be directed to the home of Miss Benevenuto.

BICICLETTA: I found the house, knocked on the door, she answered, let me in, showed me her only electric object, a many-buttoned Waring Blender, juiced up some carrots, we drank it down, them down, I gave her a rosary, thanked her and left.

POVERETTA: And then?

BICICLETTA: I hopped Bix and we rode back here.

POVERETTA: All the way back on bicycle?

BICICLETTA: Except for Indiana to Chicago on the train.

POVERETTA: A freight train?

BICICLETTA: Regular tourist super-dome. All the passengers were terribly nice about the short delay while someone helped me with Bix. Didn't you read about it in all the papers?

POVERETTA: There was nothing in the papers.

BICICLETTA: How odd.

UBBIDIENZA: We don't know how you knew this woman Lil', why you travelled the enormous distance, if in fact you did. I'm not convinced any of it happened. Proceed, Poveretta.

POVERETTA: Do you know the village of Negatano in Northern Italy?

BICICLETTA: Why can't you ask me about the pomegranates directly and for the twentieth time I will explain.

UBBIDIENZA: We are trying to prepare you.

BICICLETTA: It's premature. You think I'm a candidate for sainthood?

UBBIDIENZA: Shhh! No one said that. First comes death, then beatitude, *then* sainthood.

BICICLETTA: You're saying I'd have to die anyway, so what's this talk about preparing me for what?

UBBIDIENZA: You know your name and your deeds, if that is what they are, are known to religious the world over. It is not an epidemic, but widespread enough to have Rome direct me to conduct an investigation in a manner I see fit.

BICICLETTA: Pomegranates grow in warm sandy lands. Negatano is in the Italian Alps and neither warm nor sandy. There is a small area in the village where pomegranates thrive. The owner and gardener, Giorgio Leghorn, says he has received assistance from . . .

POVERETTA: Prayed to.

BICICLETTA: Me. I deny it. I don't know how to grow anything. And certainly not pomegranates in the Italian Alps.

POVERETTA: You receive letters from him.

BICICLETTA: Yes.

POVERETTA: You answer him.

BICICLETTA: Yes.

POVERETTA: Scientists who have examined the soil say it cannot grow pomegranates unless it has been altered and it has not been.

BICICLETTA: I admit it's a capricious miracle.

POVERETTA: Are you saying this is a miracle?

BICICLETTA: Are you?

POVERETTA: I say no.

BICICLETTA: I say yes.

CHASTITATA: Capricious dee-lishus dose pompomforgranteds.

BICICLETTA (*bowing her head*): The favorite fruit of Jesus Christ.

CHASTITATA: Ah knows de man. Ah sees Him i' sub spiritchwoll pichures. He walkin' down de abenue wid de authentic Brattleboro leathah sandals n' he suckin' on a fruit spittin' seeds right n' lef' gittin' 'em caught 'tween dusty toes when jus' den Mary Maggie cub kneelin' up tearin', "Lawdie Lawd!"

SHE sings:

Ah cries salty tears!

SHE stops singing.

Awashin' n' ascrubbin' Messianic tootsies hopin' fo' a roll i' de Sinai sand, den rubbin' n' awipin' wid de auburn tresses erotikissimo.

UBBIDIENZA: How *did* you come here?

CHASTITATA: Ah saw me dis ad i' de Jet Magazine sayin' "We Cat'licks wants you panthah sisters to leab off de unholy rollin' . . ."

Sudden switch to Yankee refinement.

You know quite clearly how I came here. I have been in convents and convent schools since I was a tot. My father was Abraham Lincoln Turner, the only black M.D. to graduate from Johns Hopkins in the whole of the teens, *and* the only doctor so trusted by the Cosa Nostra in the twenties and thirties that he was made an honorary Siciliano.

UBBIDIENZA: All right, I remember.

CHASTITATA: In 1928 when Lucky Luciano . . .

UBBIDIENZA: Stop!

SHE does.

BICICLETTA: A capricious miracle not unlike Christ's accepting the dare of Peter. "O Lord, if that is really you walking on the water, let me come out on the water too." He fell for it.

UBBIDIENZA: You mean *Peter* fell for it, fell *into* the water.

BICICLETTA: But Christ stretched forth his hand.

POVERETTA: And Bicicletta made the pomegranates grow.

BICICLETTA: Who knows?

POVERETTA: Giorgio Leghorn says he knows. How is it done?

BICICLETTA: Do you mean is there a trick?

POVERETTA: Is there?

BICICLETTA: I don't know.

POVERETTA: You don't know what?

BICICLETTA: If it's a trick. Whassamatter, cancha follo de *sin*tax?

CHASTITATA: You got dere de sin tax n' Ah gots here de poll tax. Da's de tax Ah puts on de seats o' de Polacks.

BICICLETTA: Pastor Kushinski.

UBBIDIENZA: Dead.

POVERETTA: In Salisbury, Amndesia, there is a game and bird preserve belonging to the former estate of the late Lord Blunderbuss.

BICICLETTA: Neva hoid o' de bum.

POVERETTA: In the center of this preserve is a re-creation of the Garden of Gethsemane with the statues of Jesus, Peter, and the others.

BICICLETTA: O, come now. Is this the same old crap? The statue of Christ is the only one on which the birds do not?

POVERETTA: That is Christ's doing. It has nothing to do with you.

BICICLETTA: It has to do only with Bods Odkin.

POVERETTA: You refer to the former maid of the manor on the former estate?

BICICLETTA: It's been proven that she, before dawn, rubs the statue clean. The birds do not select it for no-deposit any more than they type Shakespeare.

POVERETTA: That's monkeys.

BICICLETTA: And I'm your uncle.

POVERETTA: Bods Odkin is dead. Who now rubs the statue clean?

BICICLETTA: You tell *me*.

POVERETTA: Our Lord.

BICICLETTA: Wipes clean his own statue?

POVERETTA: Either that or the birds do not drop.

BICICLETTA: Do drop.

POVERETTA: Don't drop.

BICICLETTA: Don't drop.

POVERETTA: Do drop! All the animals in the game preserve have pink buttocks except the baboons.

BICICLETTA: The baboons are learning to ride bicycles. The black paint from the bicycle seats wears off onto their bottoms.

POVERETTA: Why then are the other animals pink?

BICICLETTA: They're not learning to ride bicycles.

UBBIDIENZA: Isn't it true, Sister Bicicletta, that they already know how?

BICICLETTA: Yes.

POVERETTA: Who taught them?

BICICLETTA: I did.

CHASTITATA: The scene. Salisbury, Amndesia. The Garden of Gethsemane, a re-creation. The statue of Jesus, kneeling, praying, sweating blood. The statues of Peter, James, others, snoring. Overhead the cockatoos, the macaws, the pelicans, the storks, the finches, the condors, and leading

them all in squadron formation the direct descendant of
the bird who, on the day of the Crucifixion, thinking to
ease The Lord's pain, plucked a thorn from the crown and
got its feathers splashed with the blood of Christ's head.
The robin redbreast! Robin Red gives the wing-down signal. SPLOOSH! Bombs away. Semper turdannis, a snow
of bird shit. Yet the statue of the Savior, the cement drops
of sweat blood aching to fall, remains unsplotched. Now
the game enter on their bicycles. The zebras, the cheetahs,
the wilde beests, the elephants, the springboks in figure
eights circling the statues, pedalling through the blizzard
as Red signals for more. Out of the bush, a family of giant
baboons in soiled morning suits and tattered evening
gowns on uni-, bi-, tri-, and tandem cycles. And bringing
up the rear of these unpinked buttocks . . .

BICICLETTA: The lovely Sassy Tallahassee from the Southern African climes.

CHASTITATA: Uhuru!

BICICLETTA: She be climbin' her bi-cycle, her feet pumpin', her legs
churnin' . . .

CHASTITATA: When, crash! Into the heart of Christ, who topples
over and crushes the cement drops of sweat blood between his beard and the earth.

BICICLETTA: Sassy Talahassee, she rip her stockings and her body
smell of bird.

UBBIDIENZA: Lord, have mercy.

POVERETTA: Lord, have mercy.

UBBIDIENZA: Lord, have mercy.

POVERETTA and CHASTITATA: Christ, have mercy.

UBBIDIENZA: Christ, have mercy.

POVERETTA, CHASTITATA and BICICLETTA: Christ, have mercy.

UBBIDIENZA: Lord, have mercy.

POVERETTA, CHASTITATA and BICICLETTA: Lord, have mercy.

UBBIDIENZA: Lord, have mercy.

CHASTITATA *and* POVERETTA *flank* UBBIDIENZA. *All three genuflect before the altar-table judge's bench. All turn right.* POVERETTA *leaves.* UBBIDIENZA *waits for* CHASTITATA *to cross in front of HER and follow* POVERETTA *off.* UBBIDIENZA *follows THEM both. This is the exit by the priest and servers at the end of the Mass.* BICICLETTA *now attends to her feet.*

SCENE FIVE.

BICICLETTA: No evil shall befall you, nor shall affliction come near your tent, for to his angels he has given command about you, that they guard you in all your ways. Upon their hands they shall bear you up.

STUZZICADENTI *enters. SHE lights a cigarette and gives it to HIM.*

Who is Brother Stuzzicadenti? What is the real Stuzzicadenti like?

STUZZICADENTI: I am in the eleventh grade. The classroom with ten minutes left in the period. Poorman looking very dapper twirling his cincture, teeth gleaming, gives us a study time. We work as he walks among the desks. He asks me, "Are you taking a little dolly to the dance tonight?" I say I am not sure. Malooley says over his shoulder, "Whassamatta, Fathah, ya jealous?" Poorman hits the boy across the face with an open hand. The boy rams against the metal bar holding the desk top to the seat. The bar snaps, the boy goes to the floor. Poorman, over him, says, "Don't you ever say that to a priest!" Later I talk to Poorman about the possibility of my vocation. He uses phone images. His calling was a busy signal or a wrong number. I ought never pick up the receiver.

BICICLETTA: Hello, Ma Bell Jesus.

Sister Stanislaus was from a visiting Order and wore white robes. In the summer, walking behind her, one could see the outline of her long body. It made me tingle and I wanted to be a nun. I wanted to cover my loveliest of legs in the white robes of Sister Stan.

It was some years before I realized my urge was thought of as *not* coming directly from God.

STUZZICADENTI: Father Poorman. The cincture. Twirl. Snap. Belt the cassock. Bunch it not too tight. Top of the shoe. Loafer. Dull shine. Eyetalian. Walk and flow. Rustle those folds and swing your robes for The Lord. Sashay sashay, let us pray let us pray.

BICICLETTA: Sister Stan. The rosary. Touch my beads. Ease them tight. Keep the white pleats pressed. Let a little stomach come forth. Just under the beads. Always just a little pregnant. Under the beads. White beads drip down the outline of Sister Stan.

STUZZICADENTI: Sashay sashay.

BICICLETTA: Let us pray let us pray.

Remember, o most gracious Virgin Mary, that never was it known, that anyone who fled to thy protection, implored thy help or sought thy intercession, was left unaided. Inspired with this confidence, I fly unto thee, o Virgin of Virgins, my mother! To thee I come before thee I stand, sinful and sorrowful. O Mother of the Word Incarnate, despise not my petition, but in thy mercy, hear and answer me.

BICICLETTA *and* STUZZICADENTI: Amen.

SCENE SIX.

POVERETTA *and* CHASTITATA.

POVERETTA: Maria Maddalena, the Sacred Vessel, carried the Eucharist on her person.

CHASTITATA: Through a band of evil boys armed with stones.

POVERETTA: She endured the abuses, the taunts.

CHASTITATA: For her maidenhead, for her faith.

POVERETTA: Though she saved the Eucharist, she lost her maidenhead.

CHASTITATA: But she did not lose her faith.

POVERETTA: And Bicicletta? She never had a maidenhead. She told me herself.

CHASTITATA: The story is well-known.

POVERETTA: Then how can she ever be a saint?

CHASTITATA: Special dispensation for the handicapped.

POVERETTA: I think the handicap is having the goddamn head in the first place.

CHASTITATA: Then have it your way. She is so favored by God he allowed her to be born without handicap.

POVERETTA: Sort of like the Immaculate . . .

CHASTITATA: Don't say it. Shh.

SCENE SEVEN.

Enter UBBIDIENZA. BICICLETTA *follows.*

UBBIDIENZA: Chastitata, you shall lead the questioning.

CHASTITATA: Gimme five, Bici.

BICICLETTA gives her "five."

Gimme ten, Cletta.

BICICLETTA gives her "ten."

You be so hip, I say gimme eleven.

BICICLETTA: Seven come and I'll put it all on a hard eight.

CHASTITATA: How many men have you been with?

BICICLETTA: At once?

CHASTITATA: Is it true at the age of three you could make the Sign of the Cross and tie your father's cravat at the same time?

BICICLETTA: I was about my father's beeswax.

CHASTITATA: Is it so that your Aunt Wanda and your Uncle Herlof . . .

BICICLETTA (*interrupting*): None of your apiary.

CHASTITATA: . . . were responsible for your late Baptism at the age of seven?

BICICLETTA (*to someone in her memory*): You promised me love-making. May I smoke?

UBBIDIENZA: Yes.

CHASTITATA: Yes.

POVERETTA: Yes.

SHE does.

CHASTITATA (*to* BICICLETTA): You have not known the joys of motherhood.

BICICLETTA: I am *capable* of having a child.

CHASTITATA: But you are not pregnant.

BICICLETTA: No.

CHASTITATA: You have been.

BICICLETTA: Three. The first time with my first husband. He didn't know. I was aborted. The second time with my second husband. He knew. I was aborted. He made me. The third time with my *second* husband. He knew. I was aborted. He made me. No times with my third husband.
  Have a child/my child/can you/I am capable
  Have a child/my child/can you/I am capable
  "Blessed is the womb that bore thee and the breasts that nursed thee"—"Rather, blessed are they who hear the word of God and keep it."

CHASTITATA: Bicicletta, your bicycle.

BICICLETTA: No one *made* me have an abortion.

BICICLETTA (*in her memory again*): I had my coat on I said goodbye to everybody twice and I still came back in so I could . . . could what . . .

If Sister had suspected I was coming during every bicycle ride, she would have taken my seat away. The amount of actual grace I received from each orgasm was enough to release ten souls from Purgatory. I decided I could give a shit if the place emptied out by April, the cruelest month anyway, we would just get rid of it once and for all.

And Jesus, Leghorn—pomegranates—why shouldn't they grow for Giorgio? He's a dear soul and he's dying quicker than most.

UBBIDIENZA: Dead.

BICICLETTA: When?

CHASTITATA: Last week. After the Mass of the Nine First Fridays.

BICICLETTA: And the pomegranates?

UBBIDIENZA produces a ripe pomegranate and sets it on the altar.

CHASTITATA: It is the last. Shall we eat it? Shall we feel its purple juices run down our throats?

BICICLETTA: Lil' Sof' Lil'?

CHASTITATA: A wen developed on her nose overnight. Ulcerous, it burst, blinding her, spilling into her outstretched mouth. She swallowed, choked and died.

BICICLETTA: When?

CHASTITATA: Wen.

BICICLETTA: When was the wen?

CHASTITATA: Last week. After the Mass of the Nine First Fridays.

BICICLETTA: In Amndesia?

CHASTITATA: Baboon Sassy Talahassee went up the hill to fetch a pail of wen juice, on her bicycle, the one you taught her to ride?

BICICLETTA: And she tried a half-gainer.

CHASTITATA: And she fell off and broke her bananas and the boon past oon.

BICICLETTA: After the Mass of the Nine First Fridays.

CHASTITATA: Leg dead Lil wenned Boon oot!

BICICLETTA: And her body smelled of bird. So much for miracles.

CHASTITATA: Sister, you have told a tale of receiving your vocation while trapped in a tree. You said a large scab had fallen off your elbow onto your knee and that you put the scab in your mouth, waited for it to dissolve . . .

BICICLETTA: Almost.

CHASTITATA: . . . and then you swallowed. As it slid down you knew that God needed you. It was not so much a calling as a buzz.

BICICLETTA: Yes.

CHASTITATA: How did you get the injury?

BICICLETTA: I fell off Bix.

CHASTITATA: You have had Bix since you were a child?

BICICLETTA: Yes.

CHASTITATA: Did you not also fall out of the tree?

BICICLETTA: No, the devil tried to saw me down, but he had the wrong branch, dumb devil, and I was saved.

CHASTITATA: Have you ever thought it might have been the devil sliding down your throat?

BICICLETTA: I do believe Lucifer exists with those other angels of light fallen from heaven, but no, he did not live in that scab.

CHASTITATA: Did he not live in that scab as much as the Body and Blood of Our Lord exists in the consecrated bread and wine?

BICICLETTA: No.

CHASTITATA: Did he not leave the outward appearances of that scab the same even as he transformed its substance into his own body and blood?

BICICLETTA: No.

CHASTITATA: Did you not swallow, Bicicletta, the transubstantiated scab, the very being of Beelzebub?

BICICLETTA: No.

CHASTITATA: Is it not so, my good Sister, that you continue to ride this excuse for a bicycle because you know you will fall, you know you will injure yourself and above all you know you will continue to consume the scabs of the very Prince of Darkness himself?

BICICLETTA: My Jesus, no!

CHASTITATA: Think on't, Bicicletta. Think on't, o Queen of scabs and patches.

UBBIDIENZA: And thou shalt renew the face of the earth. Let us pray. O God, who didst instruct the hearts of the faithful by the light of the Holy Spirit, grant that by the gift of the same Spirit, we may be always truly wise and ever rejoice in his consolation. Through Jesus Christ Our Lord.

THE THREE: Amen.

> *POVERETTA*, *CHASTITATA* and *UBBIDIENZA* do *The Mass exit.* BICICLETTA
> *goes on ballet point.*

BICICLETTA

> O that this tutu sullied point should stand
> Hold and resolve itself into a deux
> Or that the Everlasting had not fixed
> His noggin 'gainst scab-swallow. O God O God!
> How weary footed-flat and unpositionable
> Seems to me variations on this dance
> Fie on't ah fie! 'Tis an unpomegranate
> That grows no seed.

Wanda Aunt Wanda/had the closet my first husband locked me in been the closet from which you had cut off the bottom six inches to give your shoes some air I might have escaped in time for my audition/is that why dear Aunt/were you afraid your husband the walrus would lock you in/were you already planning your escape/I might have reached up and released the lock/my life might have changed/my first husband might have committed murder/

he would have been put away or executed/I never would have met him at the Albergo Fortuna/I never would have known the experience of dialing counterclockwise/dear Auntie what you have missed!

STUZZICADENTI *enters.*

STUZZICADENTI: "Show me out to slaughter," you said. Most people have left the party. I am still there and I am drunk. I scoop up another glass of champagne.

BICICLETTA: I look at your eyes and without breaking stride go past you, take a glass and turn to you.

STUZZICADENTI: We leave through a revolving door leading onto a small circular driveway. We enter an open taxi past the open gesture of the footman. The taxi departs.

BICICLETTA: You should be kissing me immediately.

STUZZICADENTI: I have just seen a man sitting on a chair pawing a woman standing before him. Disgusting, his hands, but precisely what I should be doing with mine. We say and move nothing. I want to undo my belt for relief. The taxi goes a few feet and stops. The driver puts it into reverse and goes back to the entrance of the hotel. I exit the street side. Only then am I aware that you had your hand on my right thigh. Though you didn't press, it hurt. Old sexual injury I aggravated last night when rolling over. My erection stuck me in the leg and I sprained a something. You re-enter the hotel and move to a waiting room where you lounge on a large divan. You want to play the scene over on the stage, the scene we just lived. The taxi scene. Can we get a real taxi? I move to the other rooms to search my drawers for clean drawers. An obnoxious man, God, it is the man who was pawing!, addresses you. You ask him for the taxi or at least a cutout. He replies, "Of course . . . but no."

BICICLETTA: Show me out to slaughter.

STUZZICADENTI: Yes, you said it again.

BICICLETTA: The taxi was stalled in the middle of the street. The driver Kushinski is dead. I push with all my strength and guide the taxi to the side of the curb. I prop up Kushinski on the passenger side. I sit at the wheel and think of dirty oboe duets filthy clarinet solos while in the back seat the girl with the woman's body and the rotting teeth is French-kissing the boy I want. His tongue scrapes away the jagged edges of her incisors. I have brought Dostoevski's 'The Idiot' with me and try to read of burning rubles.

STUZZICADENTI: "Then Jesus' disciples left Him and fled."

BICICLETTA: "And a certain young man was following Jesus, having a linen cloth wrapped about his naked body, and they seized him."

BICICLETTA *and* STUZZICADENTI: "But leaving the linen cloth behind he fled away from them naked."

BOTH lift their garments over their heads revealing both wearing nothing underneath, giggle and exit oppositely.

SCENE EIGHT.

POVERETTA and CHASTITATA relaxing. Frogs are heard croaking. The S.S. Pierce is being passed.

POVERETTA: At least nine saints are credited with silencing the croaking of frogs.

SHE waits. The frogs do not stop.

So much for my sainthood.

CHASTITATA: So much for miracles.

The croaking stops.

POVERETTA: Not quite.

The croaking starts.

CHASTITATA: Sts. Furseyand and Isaac spoke before birth. St. Rumwold died when three days old, but not before he recited the Apostles' Creed and preached a sermon.

The croaking stops.

POVERETTA: Is she?

CHASTITATA: A saint?

POVERETTA: Is she?

CHASTITATA: What is one?

POVERETTA: What is *two*?

CHASTITATA: What is at least nine silencing the croakings of frogs?

> *Frog croakings are heard. The sound of* BICICLETTA's *bicycle bell. The croaking stops. The bell stops.* BICICLETTA *enters.* UBBIDIENZA *beside* HER. ALL *go to their places for the next round of questioning.*

UDDIDIENZA. Do you believe in God?

BICICLETTA: The Creator of heaven and earth.

UBBIDIENZA: Do you believe in theatre?

BICICLETTA: I believe in God Theatre and Bicycle. A three-ring circusular Trinity.

UBBIDIENZA: Do you believe in Original Sin?

BICICLETTA: I believe in original-owner used bicycles.

UBBIDIENZA: Do you believe Adam and Eve lived in an entirely innocent state before the Fall?

BICICLETTA: After by Arthur Miller. I played Marilyn Monroe, her doctrine, naked, printed in calendar blood and Playboy pink.

UBBIDIENZA: Have you been considered worthless and a fool for Christ?

BICICLETTA: Who has considered me wise and prudent?

UBBIDIENZA: You know that you are discussed by cloistered religious throughout the world?

BICICLETTA: I know because you keep telling me. What about the uncloistered religious throughout the world? The ones *in* the world but not *of* it as opposed to us who are *out* of it and *not* of it.

UBBIDIENZA: When you left the theatre to enter the convent, you had just finished playing Masha in The Seagull.

BICICLETTA: I'm in mourning for my life.

UBBIDIENZA: You remarked that going from wearing black to wearing black would be like riding a bicycle after years of not. It would all come back to you.

BICICLETTA: Making love after years of making not.

UBBIDIENZA: There was enormous publicity.

BICICLETTA: The Vatican CIA hid me, then got me here. Covert convert convent.

UBBIDIENZA: Then they left you.

BICICLETTA: It was perhaps I who eluded them.

UBBIDIENZA: Why the trips? Athens, Alps, Amndesia. Did you want your cover broken?

BICICLETTA: No, and it hasn't been.

UBBIDIENZA: It has.

SHE *shows* BICICLETTA *a telegram.*

BICICLETTA: I will not meet with a journalist. Especially him.

UBBIDIENZA: Rome is allowing it.

BICICLETTA: When?

UBBIDIENZA: After I submit my report.

BICICLETTA: Does your report determine whether I am interviewed?

UBBIDIENZA: No. Holy Mother Church wants to be prepared for an onslaught.

BICICLETTA: What are you going to say?

UBBIDIENZA: What are *you* going to say?

BICICLETTA: I went to Athens, Alps, Amndesia. Next year Barcelona, Butte, Bozeman. I am called!

SHE *does the cry of the commercial.*

Call for Phillip Morrasss
I need a Camel.

UBBIDIENZA: You may not. God Theatre and Bicycle.

BICICLETTA: The boys had some foul remark about smelling bicycle seats.

UBBIDIENZA: A band of evil boys armed with stones?

BICICLETTA: I smelled mine, but it was lovely and very different.

UBBIDIENZA: There are subjects you are asked not to mention when you are interviewed. That is one of them.

BICICLETTA: I can't talk about God Theatre or Bicycle!

UBBIDIENZA: Yes, you may talk about Bicycle, but not about *sniffing* Bicycle! Do you understand?

BICICLETTA: Proceed.

UBBIDIENZA: God came down from heaven and founded a theatre. In this theatre were three rings, for every play God produced had as its setting a circus. Each play, no matter what the cries of the heart, had to climax with a naked woman in black fishnet stockings, riding a bicycle across a tight rope high above the audience with no net below. Each performance a woman fell and killed herself. Friends and relatives of God pleaded with Him to climax His plays differently, but He refused, knowing that someday a great actress and a great cyclist would appear. And one day she did.

BICICLETTA: And I think it wasn't me.

UBBIDIENZA: But what if it was you, Bicicletta, and you did not stay?

POVERETTA: "After some days He again entered Capharnaum and it was reported that He was at home. And many gathered together so that there was no longer room not even around the door. And they came bringing to him a paralytic carried by four. And since they could not bring him to Jesus because of the crowd, they stripped off the roof where He was and having made an opening, they let down the pallet on which the paralytic was lying. And Jesus, seeing their faith, said to the paralytic, 'Son, thy sins are forgiven thee.'"

CHASTITATA: "Now some of the scribes were sitting there and reasoning in their hearts, Why does this man speak thus?

He blasphemes. Who can forgive sins but only God? And at once Jesus said to them, Why are you arguing these things in your hearts? Which is easier, to say to the paralytic, 'Thy sins are forgiven thee' or to say 'Arise, take up thy pallet and walk'? And immediately the man did as he was told."

BICICLETTA: It's easier to say I think it isn't me.

UBBIDIENZA: If it is you and you did not stay, you have deserted God, not found Him. Pray for us, o Holy Mother of God.

POVERETTA *and* CHASTITATA: That we may be made worthy of the promises of Christ.

> POVERETTA, CHASTITATA *and* UBBIDIENZA *exit as at the end of* The Mass.

SCENE NINE.

BICICLETTA: I am in a play. The leading man is a star. He wants to sleep with me. I don't want him to and I don't let him. I go to that party where there are all those boys. You are there with one of all your girls. You see the star taking me into the kitchen, telling me you are a fag. I break away and come back to the bar. You are gone. That night the star has me as you know for you come in upon us with one of your many keys. We are passed out. You stand there. You tremble. You leave a note under the he-plant you call she-plant. That note, the first thing I see when I reach for my cigarettes and black Jack Daniels. I trembled too. But not as much as you.

The Lord is my Shepherd; I shall not want.

> STUZZICADENTI *enters, walking* BICICLETTA's *bicycle.*

STUZZICADENTI: I'm leaving the Order.

BICICLETTA: What Order? I thought it was a Suggestion.

STUZZICADENTI: The Sisters of the Sacred Seed and Heartbeat, Brother Division.

BICICLETTA: The Savior's mustard seed?

STUZZICADENTI: The Kingdom of Heaven is like a grain of mustard seed.

BICICLETTA: It is the smallest of all seeds, but when it grows up it is larger than any herb and becomes a tree, so that the birds of the air come and dwell in its branches.

STUZZICADENTI: But that is not the seed of our Order.

BICICLETTA: And the Heartbeat? A heartbeat away from what? The Presidency? The Divine Lap?

STUZZICADENTI: Sisters of the Savior's Buried Talents.

BICICLETTA: Aha! Now we get somewhere. Sisters of the Savior's Pulse and Passion.

STUZZICADENTI: Lord, hear our prayer.

BICICLETTA: Sisters of the Savior's Aching Flesh.

STUZZICADENTI: Lord, hear our prayer.

BICICLETTA: Sisters of the premature Crucifixion.

STUZZICADENTI: Lord, hear our prayer.

BICICLETTA: Sisters of the Christian Pecker!

STUZZICADENTI: Lord, have mercy.

BICICLETTA: You're leaving?

STUZZICADENTI: For a school bus which I will drive to and from a secondary school where I will teach Sociology to Sophomores and coach the golf squad.

BICICLETTA: You grew up on a golf course.

STUZZICADENTI: I did.

BICICLETTA: And a man you caddied for gave you a rosary.

STUZZICADENTI: He did.

BICICLETTA: I know.

STUZZICADENTI: I saw him again last night. He was sitting on a veranda outside the clubhouse. He got up and moved. I went the other way.

BICICLETTA: Because you didn't want to tell him you lost the rosary.

STUZZICADENTI: I was 19.

BICICLETTA: And the rosary came in a little pouch.

STUZZICADENTI: With a zipper.

BICICLETTA: Did you ever think the guy wanted to unzip your pouch and fuck you up the ass?

STUZZICADENTI: A man who gives me a rosary after I've caddied for him wants to do that to me? If that happened to you, you'd call it moral, mysterious.

BICICLETTA: Honest, sacred.

STUZZICADENTI: But for me . . .

BICICLETTA: It's sordid, immoral, up your ass.

STUZZICADENTI: He came around the corner I couldn't get away, but he was all head.

BICICLETTA: I bet.

STUZZICADENTI: He was just a head sitting on the ground, no, resting on normal feet.

BICICLETTA: In golf shoes.

STUZZICADENTI: Which stuck out on either side of his chin. As if what neck he had was resting on a board, a skate board which was pedalled by those feet.

BICICLETTA: Jesus, save us.

STUZZICADENTI: He asked me if he had convinced me of my vocation in The Brotherhood.

BICICLETTA: You took your golf club.

STUZZICADENTI: My putter.

BICICLETTA: You putted the skate board from under his head which dropped the two inches.

STUZZICADENTI: And bled.

BICICLETTA: And the shoes and the skate board rolled into the hole.

STUZZICADENTI: And I found the rosary in the hole.

BICICLETTA: In the zippered pouch.

STUZZICADENTI: And I prayed so hard I crushed a bead between my index finger and thumb.

BICICLETTA: Between which the priest holds the Host.

STUZZICADENTI: The priest I never am.

BICICLETTA: The virgin I never was.

STUZZICADENTI: Become a virgin.

BICICLETTA: Become a priest.

STUZZICADENTI: I'm yours in Christ.

BICICLETTA: It is He I want in me.

STUZZICADENTI: Want me.

BICICLETTA: I have seen Christ.

STUZZICADENTI: Whoopee.

BICICLETTA: I have watched Christ.

STUZZICADENTI: Making whoopee?

BICICLETTA: I have winked at Christ. Christ winked back.

STUZZICADENTI (*Handelian*): For He shall reign forever and ever.

BICICLETTA: Does He love me? Does Christ love me? He did wink back, but did He stare?
  What must I do to get you to stare at me parading down your runway? Wink my lashes off? I am on display for you I turn I gesture I dip I bow I WANT YOU UNCLE SAM JESUS!

STUZZICADENTI: Marry me.

BICICLETTA (*referring to the bicycle*): Hand over the reins of that there Trigger.

STUZZICADENTI: I'm going.

  BICICLETTA approaches the bicycle as if it were a horse.

BICICLETTA: Whoa there, boy, whoa, easy big fellow!

STUZZICADENTI: Now.

SHE has mounted the bicycle and will roar off.

BICICLETTA: Roy, you bring up the rear with Bullet.

STUZZICADENTI: Shane!

BICICLETTA: Ain't it divine, Andy? Giddyup!

SHE's off.

STUZZICADENTI: Come back, Shane, come back!

STUZZICADENTI drops to one knee, pulls out an imaginary gun and fires repeatedly.

SCENE TEN.

The Mass. UBBIDIENZA, in priest's vestments. POVERETTA and CHASTITATA to serve. BICICLETTA.

UBB: In nomine Patris et Filii et Spiritus Sancti. Amen. Introibo ad altare Dei.

BIC: I walk unto the altar of God, to God who gives joy to my youth.

POV and CHAS: Ad Deum qui laetificat juventutem meum.

UBB: Kyrie eleison.

POV and CHAS: Kyrie eleison.

Lord have mercy.

UBB: Kyrie eleison.

POV and CHAS: Christe eleison.

Christ have mercy.

UBB: Christe eleison.

POV and CHAS: Christe eleison.

Christ have mercy.

UBB: Kyrie eleison.

POV and CHAS: Kyrie eleison.

Lord have mercy.

UBB: Kyrie eleison. Dominus vobiscum.

POV and CHAS: Et cum spiritu tuo.

And with thy spirit.

UBB: Credo in unum Deum Patrem omnipotentem . . .

I believe in one God who's always invisible when you want Him around/and in His only-begotten Son begotten not made with the help of the never-virgin Bicicletta.
SHE kneels.

ET HOMO FACTUS EST.

AND WAS MADE MAN/
I reached for my cigarettes and the only thing left to drink that did not come out of a faucet the Grand Marnier/and there was your note under the he-plant you called she-plant/I am like a breath my days like passing shadows/

Et vitam venturi saeculi. Amen. Dominus Vobiscum.

POV and CHAS: Et cum spiritu tuo.

UBB: Oremus.

UBB uncovers the chalice, places the Host on the paten, and offering it up, says:

Suscipe, Sancte Pater . . .

Dominus vobiscum.

POV and CHAS: Et cum spiritu tuo.

UBB: Sursum corda

POV and CHAS: Habemus ad Dominum.

UBB: Gratias agamus Domino Deo nostro

I tell the number of the stars call each bike by name.
I must I must have you inside me and then I will draw some spiritual benefit from this scene of the offering of the bread and wine soon to become the Body and Blood of our Saviour/I will wash my hands among the innocent and will walk round Thy altar O God. Lord, I love the beauty of thy house and the place where Thy glory dwells.

You sobbed/I couldn't stop your crying and the next morning I knew you were leaving me and I told you so and you told me yes.

POV and CHAS: Dignum et justum est.

UBB: Vere dignum et justum
est. Hosanna in excelsis.

> *POV and CHAS ring the bell
> three times.*

Sanctus Sanctus Sanctus Dominus Deus Sabbaoth . . .

And the day before you suffered you took bread slivered
with wood from your carpen-
ter's hands/did you ever
really make a chair anyone
wanted to sit in/did any great
boffo furniture come out of
Nazareth/look out here
comes a miracle!

HOC EST ENIM CORPUS
MEUM

> *SHE makes the sounds of a
> dive bomber and hits
> the deck.*

> *POV and CHAS ring the
> Consecration bells*

That was a close one sure
was lucky then/another miracle like that and I'm a goner/
hit the deck!

> *POVERETTA and CHASTITATA ring the bells for the Consecration of the
> wine. BICICLETTA, again making the sounds of a dive bomber, goes for
> cover.*

UBB: Hic est enim Calix sangui-
nis mei . . .

BIC: There's bound to be
another/ miracles come in
threes

> *SHE hits the floor and waits.*

Let's see now there was the
bread changing into The
Body and then the wine

> changing into the Blood yum
> yum/maybe that's it 'til next
> time let's hear it folks, we're
> going to have ourselves a
> cann–i–ball.

BICICLETTA: Sundays and Cyball Cybele/it was a part I would have played with you only you had had amnesia.

UBBIDIENZA: Et ne nos inducas in tentationem.

POVERETTA *and* CHASTITATA: Sed libera nos a malo.

UBBIDIENZA: Amen.

UBBIDIENZA continues silently.

BICICLETTA: If only you could forget the way I was and remember that I am one of the most interesting women who has ever lived/how can you give me up/the just woman shall be glad when she sees vengeance/she shall bathe her feet in blood of the wicked but who are the wicked surely not you. And me?

UBBIDIENZA: Agnus Dei qui tollis peccata mundi, miserere nobis. Agnus Dei qui tollis peccata mundi, miserere nobis. Agnus Dei qui tollis peccata mundi, dona nobis pacem.

UBBIDIENZA says the "Domine, non sum dignus," then administers Holy Communion to POVERETTA and CHASTITATA, and to BICICLETTA. With each distribution UBBIDIENZA says the "Corpus Domini nostri." SHE then returns to the altar and continues silently.

BICICLETTA: O God why do you do this to me/why do you put yourself on my tongue/at least now I can swallow you quickly and open my mouth/when I was ten I wouldn't part my lips for a full hour after receiving you/once my mouth stuck/I forced it open and a small white dribble surely a part of the Host fell down my chin and on to my knuckle/and the time I threw up in the sacristy and I flushed the toilet and a part of the Host sat on the edge of the bowl and I wanted to wipe it up with my index finger and later I felt you wipe the last drop of sperm and put it to my mouth and I did wipe it up and I was tempted to re-eat it and I gave in and the time I received you and walking back from the Communion rail screamed to myself/FUCK THIS THING/O God why do you do this to me/ why do you put yourself on my tongue/I can't believe you like to kiss me there/and the nun's tale of the Black Massers who went to Communion at our church/Kushinski distributing Kushinski dead/the Black Massers didn't swallow the Host but put it in their handkerchiefs to take back for everyone to mock and every single time they tried when they opened their cloths there was a blood stain and nothing more/where was the Host?

UBBIDIENZA: Dominus Vobiscum.

POVERETTA *and* CHASTITATA: Et cum spiritu tuo.

UBBIDIENZA: Ite, missa est.

POVERETTA *and* CHASTITATA: Deo gratias.

SCENE ELEVEN.

UBBIDIENZA *and the Servers leave as at the end of Mass. Waltz music.* BICICLETTA *dances alone.* STUZZICADENTI *has come to watch.*

BICICLETTA: Have you left and returned?

STUZZICADENTI: I will leave after the banquet. Don't mock me.

BICICLETTA: I'm not mocking. I'm inquiring, love.

STUZZICADENTI: Don't call me love.

BICICLETTA: Have a last dance with me. Please, play another scene.

STUZZICADENTI: Your leading man will give you one last dance.

BICICLETTA: It is my line. "I left you a note."

STUZZICADENTI: "Pinned to my coat."

BICICLETTA: "With a lipstick print."

STUZZICADENTI: "And a large 'B.'"

BICICLETTA: "I told you I would return."

STUZZICADENTI: "The same night."

BICICLETTA: "I did not."

STUZZICADENTI: "And I went to one of all my girls."

BICICLETTA: "Passed out with the star under my grandmother's quilt."

STUZZICADENTI: "Under your grandmother's quilt."

BICICLETTA: "Of course."

STUZZICADENTI: "I left you a note."

BICICLETTA: "Under the he-plant."

STUZZICADENTI: "Under the she-plant."

BICICLETTA: "Some Grand Marnier."

STUZZICADENTI: "The only thing that did not come out of a faucet."

BICICLETTA: "My cigarettes."

STUZZICADENTI: "You shivered."

BICICLETTA: "But not as much as you."

STUZZICADENTI: "And the next morning . . . "

BICICLETTA: "I knew you were leaving me. And I told you so."

STUZZICADENTI: "And I told you 'yes.'"

BICICLETTA: The scene, love, that is the scene.

STUZZICADENTI: Yes, love, that is the scene.

STUZZICADENTI exits.

SCENE TWELVE.

UBBIDIENZA (*off stage*): Permesso?

BICICLETTA: Avanti.

UBBIDIENZA *enters.*

My first husband wanted an Avanti even more than a Ferrari. Lancia. Lances enter women. Arrows. Medieval. Japanese. Pornography.

UBBIDIENZA: Picasso's erotic engravings—do you think much of them?

BICICLETTA: I think a lot about them.

UBBIDIENZA: That's not the same.

BICICLETTA: Not as living them. No.

UBBIDIENZA: Are you pleased with yourself?

BICICLETTA: What are you talking about?

UBBIDIENZA: Your behavior.

BICICLETTA: My walk?

UBBIDIENZA: Your presentation. In the temple, in the chamber.

BICICLETTA: My walk.

UBBIDIENZA: Your defense. In the Chamber of Accusation.

BICICLETTA: Who designed my walk? And wouldn't you like it?

UBBIDIENZA: Are you a saint?

BICICLETTA: Yes.

UBBIDIENZA: How do you know?

BICICLETTA: Aren't you?

UBBIDIENZA: All those who die and go to heaven become saints whether formally canonized or not. But the Saint Saint is one who is prayed to, revered. One who amidst all temptations and suffering has the joy of heaven with her on earth.

BICICLETTA: That ain't me. That ain't nobody like me I ain't going to heaven I'm the first non-virgin non-martyr accused of sainthood and I ain't never going to heaven.

UBBIDIENZA: Stop saying "ain't." Confess to me.

BICICLETTA: Where's the box, the big bad confessional box?

UBBIDIENZA: We don't need one.

BICICLETTA: Perhaps not you, but me.

UBBIDIENZA: Begin.

BICICLETTA: Bless me, Madre, for I am a saint. For this sin and all the sins of my past life I am heartily sorry.

UBBIDIENZA: For your penance you must obey me. I want you to change your name. A woman of the cloth must have a holy name. "Bicycle" is not a holy name.

BICICLETTA: I'm the one who makes the name holy.

UBBIDIENZA: Theresa the Little Flower had a holy name; Agnes, Agatha, Scholastica had holy names; Perpetua and Felicitas, Catherine of Siena, Monica, St. Anne, the mother of the Blessed Virgin, Rose of Lima, Bibiana—all had holy names!

BICICLETTA: Didn't you hear me? I'm the one who makes the name Bicicletta holy. But maybe you're right. What about "Walk"? Sister Walk. Sister Andatura. I do it myself. I need no Bix with his back tire following me while I follow his front.

UBBIDIENZA: Lead *and* follow, holy woman.

BICICLETTA: No, I will always be Bicicletta. Where's the goddamn food? I am not a saint without a stomach I do not forget about my stomach I never forget I want eating every minute!

UBBIDIENZA: You're very exciting, but who could live with you? The closet-locker?

BICICLETTA: Aunt Wanda would take me in any time.

UBBIDIENZA: Or the one who stayed only as long as you were an excellent showpiece and not completely drunk? Or the one you thought too beautiful not to be a boy, who has very little courage and certainly not the courage of his lack of convictions? You still get loving notes from him, do you not?

BICICLETTA: I shiver.

UBBIDIENZA: What good are the notes?

BICICLETTA: Pink nightgown in his lap fingering me constant state Oregonasmic lose consciousness in my mouth.

UBBIDIENZA: You got your shivering body into his.

BICICLETTA: Even my gut. My gut hangs out when it is not in French kisses.

UBBIDIENZA: I want some. I want to be like you.

BICICLETTA: I love the way people like me. Pastor Kushinski!

UBBIDIENZA: Dead!

BICICLETTA: Pushing car/no one in it to brake

UBBIDIENZA: Bicicletta, my charge . . .

BICICLETTA: Charge me.

UBBIDIENZA: With obedience.

BICICLETTA: Obedience.

UBBIDIENZA: Poverty.

BICICLETTA: Chastity.

UBBIDIENZA: As Holy Mother Church . . .

BICICLETTA: . . . sees fit.

UBBIDIENZA: Make my memories.

BICICLETTA: Pushing car/no one in it to brake/starts to get away/ fall/hold on to bumper/car pops its own clutch/starts itself/mouth locked around exhaust/slide along.

UBBIDIENZA: No despair. Hope. As Holy Mother Church . . .

BICICLETTA: . . . sees fit.

UBBIDIENZA: Eat now.

BICICLETTA: My gut hangs down, sucked in by French kisses. I need too many memories.

UBBIDIENZA: Make mine for me.

BICICLETTA: I don't see fit. Eat.

UBBIDIENZA: Let us eat. In hope.

SCENE THIRTEEN.

Country-rock music. POVERETTA *and* CHASTITATA *yelling "Mangiamo."*
BICICLETTA *and* UBBIDIENZA *move to* THEM. *Dancing. The altar-table has
become a smorgasbord.* STUZZICADENTI *setting out plates and trays and
the ever-present S. S. Pierce.* BICICLETTA *hurls HERself into dance.*
UBBIDIENZA *trails on.*

UBBIDIENZA: Bicicletta, mangia mangia!

CHASTITATA: Bicicletta, eat my heart out!

POVERETTA: Bicicletta, lie with me!

UBBIDIENZA: Bicicletta, remember your gut!

CHASTITATA: Bicicletta, this crazy nigger wants you!

POVERETTA: Bicicletta, lie with us!

UBBIDIENZA: Bicicletta, give me French kisses!

CHASTITATA: Bicicletta, touch this crazy nigger!

POVERETTA: Bicicletta, lie with all of us!

UBBIDIENZA: Bicicletta, your body shivers!

CHASTITATA: Bicicletta, give up that thing!

POVERETTA: Bicicletta, lie lie lie!

BICICLETTA: I don't want any of you crazy niggers!

BICICLETTA breaks away and says this to none of THEM.

Don't hate me for those proper shoes I couldn't find, those
proper feet which weren't mine. That hillbilly bar I kept
dragging you and everybody else to. I'm going out for
cigarettes. That's what I told you. The first time you
believed me. Don't dislike me, love. You're bored. My
dumb actions. Don't dislike me. I can't help it. I can, but I
don't want to and I don't I don't do it help it I couldn't
believe it. Stop saying "it"! I can't help.

*BICICLETTA goes to the food and gorges HERself. SHE hoists the S.S.
Pierce, throws it to her mouth and pours half of it down her dress. As
quickly as SHE began stuffing down everything SHE now stops
completely. SHE races off.*

SCENE FOURTEEN.

*BICICLETTA enters her room. SHE will remove her wet clothing, sponge
the top half of her body, shave her legs with a dry razor, cut herself
once and put on black fishnet stockings and a white trenchcoat to cover
her nakedness.*

BICICLETTA: Bix buddy, we're going to roll out of here real smooth
and onto that high wire.

I had to get your attention you were on the phone so I
got the razor and shaved my legs in front of you. I put
them up on your seat as I had in the third grade my
loveliest of limbs and made them bleed in front of you. I
lifted my arm to shave the pit finally you paid attention to
me but I cut clean the hair anyway. When I lifted the other
arm you shouted "No" and I pulled the phone cord out of
the wall. As you too late reached to stop me I cut clean the
other underarm hair. I then put a dress on over nothing
and we went to a drunken bullshit where everybody made
speeches praising the theatre. The next day as we were on
location staging the parade, I hid in the bar drinking Cour-
voisier and crying. I was crying for the theatre. Remember
the scene? The theatre is going under. In the play, that is.
The theatre is broke. No solution. The stage manager gets
an idea. He gathers all the townspeople, every last one of
them, and this spontaneous—HAH!—how they were all
rehearsed!, outpouring of support for the theatre saves
the day. As I saw all these people in this play, in this play
about how to save the theatre, I had to cry. Nobody will
save the theatre. No spontaneous outpouring will ever
gather to save any theatre! In fact we weren't even in a
play. We were doing the goddamn thing on *television*!

> Have a child/my child/can you?
> I am the Bride of Christ and this is our wedding night.
> In God's theatre I will become a virgin.
> The Eucharist will be my maidenhead.

SHE goes to her bicycle.

C'mon, Bix m'man, The Big Top awaits.

SHE mounts the bicycle and rides out the door.

SCENE FIFTEEN.

BICICLETTA on her bicycle.

BICICLETTA: My God, we are making love. I watch you as you go
down my body, I hold the sheet above my head, close it
behind my neck and make a tent for us. I now believe you
like to kiss me there. You come back to my mouth and
slide yourself between my teeth. I feel a bewildered look
take over my face as if I can't believe we are going on
together. You rub past my cheek as I hold and give you a
final lick, then down you go and penetrate.

EPILOGUE.

*POVERETTA and CHASTITATA asleep in each other's arms. UBBIDIENZA
praying.*

UBBIDIENZA: God, in Your infinite wisdom and perspective, You
prove Your own existence through design—the design of
Your own theatre. In Your theatre there is only one seat.
All the lines of sight are perfect. As soon as Bicicletta
comes onto the rope, You can see directly up her fishnet
tights and beyond. But You cannot linger, for thighs flash
and even You must look upon a blur. God, You are good.
We thank You for the Theatre of Flashing Thighs and the
life Your Son Our Lord has found in our Bicicletta.

Hail Holy Queen Mother of Mercy, our life our sweet-
ness and our hope, to thee do we cry, poor banished
children of Eve; to thee do we send up our sighs, mourning and weeping in this valley of tears. Turn then, o most
gracious advocate, thine eyes of mercy towards us; and
after this, our exile, show unto us the blessed fruit of thy
womb, Jesus. O clement, o loving, o sweet Virgin Mary.

*BICICLETTA has entered during the final section. Her coat is on, but
SHE's a bit of a mess. STUZZICADENTI, suitcase in hand, comes on after.*

BICICLETTA: Pray for us, o Holy Mother of God.

UBBIDIENZA: That we may be made worthy of the promises of Christ.

STUZZICADENTI: Who do you think you are? St. Blandina?

BICICLETTA: No.

STUZZICADENTI: St. Cecilia?

BICICLETTA: No.

STUZZICADENTI: St. Agnes?

BICICLETTA: No.

STUZZICADENTI: St. Febronia of Sibapte?

BICICLETTA: I could give a shit for St. Febronia of Sibapte.

UBBIDIENZA: Let us pray. O God, our refuge and our strength, look down in mercy on thy people who cry to Thee: and by the intercession of thy glorious and immaculate Virgin Mary, Mother of God, of St. Joseph, her spouse, of thy blessed Apostles Peter and Paul and of all the saints, in mercy and in goodness hear our prayers for the conversion of sinners and for the liberty and exaltation of our holy mother the Church. Through the same Christ Our Lord.

BICICLETTA: Amen.

STUZZICADENTI: Why did you keep shouting . . .

BICICLETTA: I am now a virgin! I carry the Eucharist!

STUZZICADENTI: Riding naked through the streets crying "I am now a virgin. I carry the Eucharist!"? Where is it?

BICICLETTA: Where? I am capable of having a child, but I will not have one. I will have the Eucharist.

UBBIDIENZA: Holy Michael, the archangel, defend us in battle: be our safeguard against the wickedness and snares of the devil. May God rebuke him, we humbly pray; and do thou, prince of the heavenly host, by the power of God cast into hell Satan and the other evil spirits, who wander through the world seeking the ruin of souls.

BICICLETTA: Amen.

UBBIDIENZA: Most Sacred Heart of Jesus.

BICICLETTA: Have mercy on us.

STUZZICADENTI: Bicicletta.

UBBIDIENZA: Most Sacred Heart of Jesus.

BICICLETTA: Have mercy on us.

STUZZICADENTI: Bicicletta.

UBBIDIENZA: Most Sacred Heart of Jesus.

BICICLETTA: Have mercy on us.

STUZZICADENTI: Bicicletta.

FINITO.

Necktie Party

THE PLAYERS:

EARL COLT
DONALD WINCHESTER
ALICE COLT WINCHESTER
EVANESCENT WILCOX WINCHESTER COLT
FATHER

TIME:
1987

DONALD: Today I stole a book from the New York University Book Store. I was not caught. I had de-sensitized the book with a special de-sensitizer I have developed myself. I put the book in my pocket, passed through the archway detector (by the time I have to wear a pacemaker I shall have to come up with a different scheme), the beeper did not go off and I stepped out into the perfection of the afternoon light.

ALICE: Today I stole a book from the New York University Book Store. I was stopped by a security guard, a woman named Beatrice, before I could pass through the archway detector. Beatrice said she would have to examine the books in my pockets.

EARL: Today I was accused of stealing a book from the New York University Book Store. I had gone into the store and through the turnstiles and was standing at the sale book counter when I realized that I had two books in my outside pockets, both of which books, the tops, were visible if anyone cared to look.

EVANESCENT: Beatrice cared.

ALICE: I handed over both books without fear because I had desensitized them with my own specially patented desensitizer and knew they would not set off any alarm. Correction: I had stolen one of the books at a country store which had no detection system and carried it with me into the NYU store to complicate the matter if I were stopped.

EARL: I thought that I should go back through the turnstiles, put both books, one which I had purchased at a country store the week before and the other which I had purchased the day before at the NYU Book Store, into the lockers provided for personal belongings. Or perhaps I should look for the nearest security person and tell that person what I had just realized. The thought lasted a split-second.

ALICE: I said to Beatrice, "Isn't that funny? No sooner had I pushed through the turnstiles when I realized I had two books with me, one of which I'd be very surprised if you sell, this book of Czechoslovak poetry, and the other which you do sell, Teach Yourself Polish, which I purchased here just yesterday."

EARL: I continued through the store, picked up a sale item—"The Plebeians Rehearse the Uprising" by Günter Grass—a notebook, 120 sheets, college-ruled, three sections and proceeded to the cash register. As I was paying, I noticed the security woman waiting on the other side of the counter. Waiting, or so it seemed. It occurred to me that the books in my pocket might mean trouble. Another split-second.

ALICE: Beatrice took both books and walked through the archway detector.

EVANESCENT: The alarm did not go off.

EARL: As I was pulling out my money, I saw the girl at the cash register take the sale book, "The Plebeians, etc." and run the spine of it back and forth three times over a rectangular box. I had watched this done before but this was the first time I paid special attention to it.

ALICE: Beatrice then said she would not give me back my books unless I produced a receipt. I quite calmly explained that I had purchased the poetry book elsewhere (I refrained from saying that her shitty little book store is not hip enough to know this book exists) and that I had purchased the Teach Yourself book the day before. Yes, she had now heard this twice.

EARL: I took my purchases, and the books in my pockets of course, and approached the archway.

EVANESCENT: "I'm going to have to see the books in your pockets," said the black trench-coated Beatrice.

ALICE: She insisted she would not release the books until I had produced a receipt. I said I had no intention of producing receipts for purchases I had made in the past, that the fact that the alarm system had not gone off, indicating no proof whatsoever that I had stolen either book, exonerated me in a society whose legal system presumed innocence and furthermore I demanded that she return my books immediately or I would institute legal action.

EARL: I handed both books to this middle-aged pop-up cop I had seen a thousand times and explained why I had them in my pockets, even detailing my split-second doubts after I had entered the store. She said she had seen me many times before and knew I was a good customer. She walked through the detector, it did not beep, then she insisted upon a receipt. I said, "I don't carry receipts for past purchases and if I'm such a good customer, which indeed I am," I'm on the bloody faculty and I order hundreds of books through the store each year, I didn't tell her I was on the faculty, I was not trying to pull rank, "why don't you believe me?"

EVANESCENT (*to ALICE*): "Store policy demands a receipt. No receipts, no books."

EARL: She took my books back to a video terminal and had someone there punch them up. I once again tried to explain to her that the presence of these books in my pockets had been completely inadvertent. She handed me the book of Czechoslovak poetry.

EVANESCENT: "We do not sell this book."

EARL: I told her once again I had purchased it elsewhere. She held up the Teach Yourself Polish book.

EVANESCENT: "But we do sell this."

EARL: I told her that I had told her that and that I had purchased it the day before.

EVANESCENT: "No receipt, no book."

EARL: She went toward the cash registers. I stormed after her and raised my voice.

ALICE: And raised my voice.

EARL: I picked up the rectangular box just as the girl at the cash register was running the spine of a book over it.

EARL *and* ALICE: What is this box for? What is that detection archway for? Does none of it work? Is it only here to fool customers into thinking there *is* a security system?

EVANESCENT: In the quietest mouse-squeakingest voice she said, "Sometimes it doesn't work."

EARL: You can say that again, sweetheart.

DONALD: The CatchasCatchCan agency will burglarize your apartment for only $195 or else we will sell you a sticker for $5 that you put on your door which says which *says* we have burglarized your home. Or is it de-burglarized?

EARL *and* ALICE: I demand to see the Director.

EVANESCENT: "I'll see if I can find her."
        "I'm the Director of the Book Store and we've had words before, haven't we?"

ALICE: I beg your pardon—

EARL: We have had no words before.

EVANESCENT: "I'm going to make an exception in this case."

EARL: Make no exceptions. That says you are pardoning me for a crime. I have committed no crime.

EVANESCENT: "Let me explain to you our store policy."

EARL *and* ALICE: I know what the store policy is.

EVANESCENT: "We live in a kind of society—"

EARL *and* ALICE: I know what kind of society we live in.

EVANESCENT: "Are you a student?"

EARL *and* ALICE: I'm 106 years old and I'm on the fucking faculty.

EVANESCENT: "Normally our procedure is prosecution, but I'm going to make an exception in this case and let Mrs. Beatrice or whatever the hell her name is, let you leave the store with this book."

EARL *and* ALICE: I don't want exceptions for faculty. If President Brademas himself steals a book, he ought to be prosecuted.

EVANESCENT: "Ha ha ho ho, well wouldn't that be an event?"

EARL *and* ALICE: O, you've had words with him in the past, have you?

EVANESCENT: "There is absolutely no way we can prove you did not steal the book."

EARL: That logic has its head up its ass.

ALICE: You have to prove that we *did* steal the book.

EVANESCENT: "If you wish, you may continue on with your shop-
ping."

EARL *and* ALICE: Not bloody likely.

The alarm system goes off.

EVANESCENT: "See, it does go off!"

EARL: Took you long enough to find the button.

DONALD: The person who possesses the most books has the most
power. Power is exponentially related to book-owning. I
realize I have never known what "exponential" means, but
I do know what a book is and now I'm realizing its power.
If I possessed every book in the New York University
Book Store, if I de-sensitized every book in the New York
University library—how long would it take me to walk out
of the library carrying each and every de-sensitized volume, I'd have to do it myself, I couldn't trust anybody, I'd
have to be the only thief working with me; if I took every
book from every store and library in New York, I am 45,
five years of continual de-sensitizing and walking out, I
could brook no accomplices, if I had in my possession,
exponentially, every book in New York City, would I not
be, I *would* be the most powerful shit in the world! I could
trump Trump, turn off Turner, stick it up Murdoch's
whazoo. I would control what was published, I'd have to
do Boston too, I'd make no pretense about leaving edito-
rial boards intact, I'd wipe them all out and once a year I'd
invite *my* people to *my* library of *my* most precious posses-
sions, numbering a round million volumes which would
reach up 25, 50 stories, whatever it would take, surround-
ing an atrium, with a pool of boiling blood in the center of
the center, into which I would dunk, holding each by one
heel, every pisshead and shit-eyed book store pop-up cop
and Die-rector.

EARL: The experience made me want to become a criminal.

ALICE: It made me continue being a criminal.

DONALD: I've never not been a criminal.

EVANESCENT: If there were no book thieves, Beatrice would be unemployed and would most certainly turn to crime.

ALL FOUR: We work in an Unemployment Office where we help the unemployed find jobs. The unemployed, like the poor, O Jesus Christ, are always with us. Even if everyone had a job, not everyone would have a job, for we, the finders of jobs for people with no jobs, would have no jobs.

DONALD: Not one of us can prove that she or he is not a criminal. It is the goal of our society, in which the Book Store Director is Queen, to show us all that we can never demonstrate our honesty.

ALICE: Integrity resides within, but who can possibly care even a small shit? It is without, outside, what people see that makes the difference, and if the only thing on the outside, the only thing people see, is the *not* and the *not* . . .

EVANESCENT: "We can *not* prove that you did *not* steal the book."

ALICE: The cause of integrity is doomed.

DONALD: So, why try?

ALICE: The course of true integrity never did run.

EARL: Wasn't there a moment when Beatrice or Director wanted just to stop and say, "This is absurd, this man didn't steal this book. We're terribly sorry and have a nice life."

DONALD *and* ALICE: No.

EVANESCENT: No.

EARL: Do they still earnestly, oh earnestly, believe that I stole the book?

DONALD *and* ALICE: Yes.

EVANESCENT: Yes.

EARL: Do they think about it at all?

DONALD *and* ALICE: No.

EVANESCENT: Yes.

EARL: We have contracts, we have negotiations, handshakes, words (we've had words before, I'd be happy to take you

to lunch) we have trust, faith, belief, confidence (confi-
dence rackets, in God we trust, all others pay cash)—
  Sign at the city limits of Macon, Georgia—
    Nigger, if you can read this, run.
    If you can't read this, run anyway
  My name is Earl Colt and I'm forty-five today.

DONALD: I'm Donald Winchester and I'm forty-five today.

ALICE: I'm Alice Colt Winchester and this is my birthday party
for these gentlemen.

EVANESCENT: My name is Evanescent Wilcox Winchester Colt and
I'm here for the ride.

DONALD sings "Splish Splash" à la Bobby Darin

DONALD: I was a sophomore, '60, '61, God was dead around then,
wasn't He?

EARL: God thinks He's a black lesbian.

ALICE: No, she doesn't and God wasn't dead until Time Magazine's cover proclaimed same in 1963.

EVANESCENT: November 22.

DONALD: I had *no* money.

EARL: A college student without money is not a guy living in a
box on a bench in Battery Park.

DONALD: I started stealing food every day from the A & P.

EARL: "Excuse me, young man, how do you expect me to make a
profit when you're paying for one can of Campbell's Ched-
dar Cheese soup and stealing a 16 oz. packet of bologna
and two sticks of butter?"

DONALD: I don't expect you to make a profit, that is, I don't think
anything about profits, unless they're Old Testament
prophets in my theology course, Advanced Justice for an
Ethical Era.

EARL: "I've called the police. What they're going to do with you,
take you downtown, book you, demand your draft card
. . ."

ALICE: No one was burning them yet.

EVANESCENT: Guys bought fake ones to be used as i.d.'s to buy booze.

EARL: "I don't know, but this could give you a criminal record."

ALICE: And keep you out of the draft.

DONALD: Of course, I wasn't thinking that way.

EARL: You were scared shitless.

DONALD: The cops came and they didn't take me downtown, but to the Dean of Men.

EARL: A giant guy name of Tinkle.

DONALD: And nobody messed with Dean Tinkle, who put me on Social Probation, meaning I was not allowed to contract disease for a whole semester, and then I wrote him a sonnet about how guilty I felt and he re-instated me to full graces, sanctifying, actual, comical, historical—

ALICE: Ah—

EARL: Ah—

EVANESCENT: Did he tell your father?

EARL (as Claudius)
> "'Tis sweet and commendable in your nature, Hamlet,
> To give these mourning duties to your father;
> But you must know, your father lost a father;
> That father lost, lost his, and the survivor bound
> In filial obligation for some term
> To do obsequious sorrow. But to persever
> In obstinate condolment is a course
> Of impious stubbornness. 'Tis unmanly grief."

DONALD: 'Tis unmanly grief.

EVANESCENT: He used to have a punch bag in the basement
> hit that bag
> and there
> then
> the was
> the Camels
> and the bathroom and the shit on the wall

and Camel smoke it's ah
in my nose
Stockyards
my nostrils
now
it it shit the shit and the smoke
smoke toke in the warsh-room
Warshington my he
and Camels' smoke
shh smoke shit smoken-shit
and his shirts like and the Camel shit and the smoke
punch bag
Stockyards
in the basement
nose jam shittn' smoke
Camel pack in shirt pock
sock hose sock nose
feet shit smoke toes
smoke nose

EARL, EVANESCENT.

EVANESCENT: My old man's dead and he does it well. He's full of great dead.

EARL: No Sixties stuff. This is your slave name?

EVANESCENT: I beg your pardon?

EARL: Evanescent Wilcox your slave name?

EVANESCENT: It's my owner name.

EARL: Owner's name.

EVANESCENT: No, *owner* name. I own it.

EARL: Yes'm. Now divest yourself of your South African holdings and take off your clothes.

EVANESCENT: I'm not ready.

EARL: My dear heart, I note the bruised veins about your well make-upped eyelids, I have seen the flare of your pitted-out nostrils, I have shaken your hand with the cigarette burns on it and I now tell you are ready.

ALICE, DONALD.

ALICE: I was in the hall. I heard you coming down the stairs so I slipped into a room. I knew if I saw you too soon I'd lose you.

DONALD: I passed the room and you came out a second later.

ALICE: I needed to avoid you for just that second.

DONALD: I thought you'd been looking at yourself in the full-length mirror behind the door.

ALICE: No, I'd been saving our lives.

ALICE.

ALICE:
Daddy say let me in Sugar and Sugar say no
so Daddy go 'way I play all day
I leave
Daddy come go in say words I hear not too clear
smear/I cheer Daddy Dad/beer beer/Daddy leave/
I need pee I in go
smear poo Daddy smear poo over every/
poo on potty/poo on sink/poo on tub/drink drink drink/
beer on potty/beer on sink/beer on tub/stink stink 'frow up/
Daddy smear why/Daddy beer/poo on mirror/poo on birror/
poo on wall/all all all/
'frow up 'frow up on the wall Daddy pooest of them all

ALICE, EVANESCENT.

ALICE: Lamb's placenta. Pulled through every strand. For treatment of damaged hair.

EVANESCENT: Jism to bind back together my loose ends.

ALICE: We must needs be so arranged.

EVANESCENT: We be so arranged.

ALICE: Un-mussed and fussed over.

EVANESCENT: Un-shushed and blown dry.

ALICE: Do, do hold my wrap, Eternal Footman.

EVANESCENT: Lynchman.

ALICE: I've won! What great good fortune! Yes, I'll be there to accept the award. Oh, thank you, kind sir and madam. What a great thrill for me after all these years of hardest work and gruel and grueling disappointment—to be on top. And, yes, I'll give a little speech.

EVANESCENT: How much? How many? How high? How often? How low? How many times? How much? That's better. That's right, guy, I'm a veteran, but I ain't giving no speeches.

ALICE: Oh, what will I wear? I must shop.

EVANESCENT: The silk. It slides down and off and leaves no marks.

ALICE: My wrap. My wrap!

EVANESCENT: I'll do this until the money stops or you don't notice me or both.

ALICE: Just think—

EVANESCENT: With tongue up asshole.

ALICE: Just think—

EVANESCENT: So far.

ALICE: I won!

EVANESCENT: I don't work, I go to parties.

ALICE: My entire career, and people will be there—everybody who's always loved me.

EVANESCENT: They don't love, they shove.

ALICE: Will see me, see me up there.

EVANESCENT: With silk sliding down and leaving no marks.

ALICE: You'll be in the back, Eternal Man.

EVANESCENT: I'll be in the back with the noose, tongue up his everywhere.

ALICE: Holding my coat.

EVANESCENT: Brushing lamb placenta, sheep jism into your fur-est of collars.

ALICE: And my speech, my little speech!

EVANESCENT: My reward.

ALICE: In my softest of hands I'll be holding my words.

EVANESCENT: In my rust-stained hands I'll be holding my, my wash-erwoman hands.

ALICE: My soft words of thanksgiving.

EVANESCENT: My Bible school prayers through the cigarette burns.

ALICE: My kind, my gentle words, o thank you, kind sirs and madams, for this honor that I've really won at last.

EVANESCENT: The Lord of human bondage shall tie my hands be-hind his back and hang me there to dry his tie.

ALICE: O, Lord, I've won at last. Won, won at last!

EVANESCENT: Your coat, ma'am.

EARL, DONALD.

EARL: You have the white man's disease.

DONALD: There's only one?

EARL: You can't jump.

DONALD: Me and Larry Bird.

EARL: You don't think with your thighs.

DONALD: You're right, you don't think with your thighs.

EARL: *You* don't.

DONALD: And the roundness of your ass.

EARL: The lift from the buns and the bunlets.

DONALD: The tibia or fibia up from your ankles into your calves.

EARL: The stretch factor.

DONALD: The slave-slamdunk sexuality of both feet through the hoop.

EARL: Hover Man, I'm the Hover Man. You, little white man, Antarctic white, white-on—

DONALD: White on!

EARL: I need super dark shades to look at you even askance.

DONALD: I would blind you all.

EARL: You would not let me shit shower shave or shampoo.

DONALD: I put the lye in your Dixie Peach.

EARL: You give us the lie in the throat as deep as to the lungs.

DONALD: We gonna pluck off your mustache, blow it in your face and see where your strength be then, Sambo.

EARL: We gonna grab you where your tail should be and twirl you 'round 'til your butter fall off.

DONALD: With arms so long—

EARL: I boxed God to a draw.

DONALD: With arms so long no shirt of yours alive's more than short sleeve.

EARL: Arms and the man. The People's Liberation Army.

DONALD: The Simianese Liberation Army. Take us on out, KoKo.

ALICE, EVANESCENT.

ALICE: She who can say how she burns, burns little—Petrarch.

EVANESCENT: Who?

ALICE: It's while it's being lived that life's still immortal, that it's still alive—Marguerite Duras.

EVANESCENT: Take me to the theater again.

ALICE: I hope not.

EVANESCENT: O, to see you leaping the seats to get to that albino.

ALICE: O—

EVANESCENT: While life's still immortal.

ALICE: When I do it—

EVANESCENT: When you steeplechase after those lame grey-
hounds—

ALICE: An error of Prussian proportions. For love, love—love.

EVANESCENT: She who can say how she burns, burns little, and
Petrarch ain't no she.

ALICE: No.

EVANESCENT: *He* wrote *he.*

ALICE: Yes.

EVANESCENT: You changed 'it' to 'she.'

ALICE: I changed 'he' to 'she.'

EVANESCENT: Why are we so worried about gender, when they
don't care? Why are we we and they they?

ALICE: I sure did leap.

EVANESCENT: Not quite.

ALICE: Why did you stop me?

EVANESCENT: Somebody had to.

ALICE: Why did *somebody have* to?

EVANESCENT: What was his name?

ALICE: Bugge.

EVANESCENT: Boogie?

ALICE: No. Bugge. B-u-g-g-e. John Bugge. German. Prussian.

EVANESCENT: Mercedes. That time Donald was out.

ALICE: Earl was out.

EVANESCENT: You were on the phone with Mr. Boogedy.

ALICE: You wouldn't leave me be.

EVANESCENT: After the leaping.

ALICE: Right after.

EVANESCENT: Alice, Alice, what kind of food should we order out?

ALICE: Japonais.

EVANESCENT: Raw—raw—

ALICE: How—

EVANESCENT: How do we free ourselves?

ALICE: Feel ourselves.

EVANESCENT: Feel free.

ALICE: From these albinos.

EVANESCENT: From this leaping—

ALICE: Over seats. In the theater of our burns.

EVANESCENT: Burn little.

DONALD.

DONALD:
An exposition expedition exhibition
mah Daddy 'sposin' hisself downtown Navy Poo Pier
ChiChicago Shitcago 'sposin' Ah was 'sposin' mahself
World's Fair type of 'sposin' hisself he was 'sposin'
both selfs holdin' mah thingaling smack me upside the dinga-
        ling
we be exhibited no *in*hibited *out*hibited we walkin' 'long
with our little 'rections defyin' the gravitational pull of the
moontide riptide let 'er rip Daddy/ Daddy get faint sit down
on curb tell only number only son he restin' up so go 'way
let Daddypoo rest up thing and maybe have a little attack to
        boot/
clutch chest/I move on wait for Daddy/hold own thing/
people look/I cry/Daddy rest up for next attack

EVANESCENT, ALICE, EARL.

EVANESCENT: Daddy died.

ALICE: My Daddy died.

EARL: Well, sweet little Nefertitis, no more Daddy, huh?

EVANESCENT: I be five and Daddy have me on his knee and Daddy
        flip me all over under, Flip Daddy, and there be pennies

from Daddy's heaven and nickels from Daddy's nuts, dimes from Daddy's diamonds, family jewels, and two quarters from Daddy's I don't know where and I be playing with *all* this money, sliding it up and around, coin flip-flopping—

ALICE: I need my own money, I need to earn it, I don't care if I earn it, I need it I need it.

EVANESCENT: I be five and Daddy have me on his knee and Daddy flip.

ALICE: I need my own support because even after death Daddy will hold it against me.

EVANESCENT: Flip! In my mouth a penny, nickel, dime, oh no, a quarter I swallow whole I choke.

ALICE: I fall on the quarters of life, I choke I choke.

EVANESCENT: Daddy rush me to hospital and by now I swallow everything bawling and bawling and Doctor say this too shall pass this too shall pass.

ALICE: If I don't have my own money, if I use Daddy's money, he will never give it no strings attached, if I use it, he will come back, fucking ghost that he be—

EVANESCENT: Fucking ghost that he be.

ALICE: And he's going to say—You can all shutthefuck up, 'cause *I* make the money. I make all the money and I make *all* the decisions.

EVANESCENT: And that little roll of penny, nickel, dime and quarter passed down and out, we examined it close up, we got our fingers way in it and saw the hard-earned, hard-swallowed money of my Daddy in my Daddy's daughter's shit.

The Interrogation.

EARL, DONALD.

EARL: Happiness.

DONALD: A warm censorship.

EARL: Yesterday it was fragility.

DONALD: Frugality.

EARL: Fragility.

DONALD: Frigidity.

EARL: The way you described her condition.

DONALD: The welder's son.

EARL: She called you the welder's son. You then identified her condition as frigidity.

ALICE in.

ALICE: It's a filthy word.

DONALD: False.

ALICE: Not false.

DONALD: It's a filthy false word.

EARL: Nonetheless—

DONALD: I used it. She had never come.

ALICE out.

EARL: Until?

DONALD: I don't know. Perhaps it's not until but unless. I used the word to hurt her.

EARL: Why are you admitting this to me?

DONALD: I don't believe you'll punish me anymore if I confess, excuse me, admit, my crimes of romance.

EARL: Pecker-dilloes.

DONALD: Thank you.

EARL: You wrote it.

DONALD: The word? Ages ago, I suppose.

EARL: Encased in the filth, the falsehood.

DONALD: I hurt her other ways. I said *this* was wrong with her appearance, *that* marred my appreciation of her.

EARL: Racism.

DONALD: Probably.

EARL: Definitely.

DONALD: Believe what you want.

EARL: I believe what you're telling me, directly and indirectly. Is writing more important to you than death?

DONALD: The correct answer to that is unclear to me.

EARL: You won't get anywhere with me quoting me.

DONALD: You'll admit it was quoting, it was not extrapolating.

EARL: Writing used to be more important to you than death. Is it now?

DONALD: Writing is not very important at all; even less so death.

EARL: Do you call your attitude courageous?

DONALD: I don't *call* it anything. I'm not Adam. I don't name the animals.

EARL: You name us monkeys.

DONALD: Not even when I hated you.

EARL: You called her Zippie the Chimp.

DONALD: You have that on tape.

EARL: With perfect clarity.

DONALD: Well—it was what or whom she called herself.

EARL: We don't have that on tape.

DONALD: What are you going to do with me?

EARL: Even if this is cat and mouse, what difference does it make to you? You don't care for writing, even though you present yourself to the world as someone who does. You don't care for life, even less so than you care for writing. What is it that moves you?

DONALD: Bran.

EARL: You've seldom been clever enough.

DONALD: What keeps me alive is my ability to write speeches for you. The time I am clever enough is time enough, seldom though it may be, whereas you are never.

DONALD out. ALICE in.

EARL: When? When she has her tongue so far up my asshole—

ALICE: Excuse me?

EARL: Excuse *me*. Trying to write. Turning a phrase—when her tongue she has, when her tongue has she—

ALICE: I think sex should be enjoyed, not written about.

EARL: I think sex should be written about, not enjoyed.

ALICE: So practiced, so rehearsed. So un-done. If it didn't happen by the time I was thirty-five—

EARL: And it didn't.

ALICE: Are you asking or telling?

EARL: I don't have to ask.

ALICE: Smug shit.
It's not going to.

EARL: The "it" of orgasm, the genderless explosion.

ALICE: The literature insists that men come when hanged.

EARL: Upon pain of death. I believe it.

ALICE: My whole sex life passing before me. Drowning in the noose. I'm a magnificent swimmer, but—

EARL: You give great swim.

ALICE: When the phones worked—

EARL: They work.

ALICE: When they worked, were you one of those making those calls?

EARL: You mean—Wouldn't you like to perform this or that on me?

ALICE: Through the wires. When the phones worked.

EARL: Everything works.

ALICE: In your newly re-named land, what's it called? Everything works except for a small problem now and then with the water supply. Plutonium, feces, gun powder.

EARL: Not so long ago—

ALICE: Midnight. You called. Wanted my tongue.

EARL: Cigarette-burned.

DONALD, EVANESCENT.

DONALD: Back again?

EVANESCENT: Fourth or fifth time.

DONALD: Can't stay away.

EVANESCENT: You haven't had time to call me, have you?

DONALD: I have the number and I'm to call after seven.

EVANESCENT: Not the same one I gave you and you can call anytime.

DONALD: I *haven't* had time.

EVANESCENT: I was giving you your excuse.

DONALD: Aren't you his woman?

EVANESCENT: Whose?

DONALD: Did you say you'd kill him?

EVANESCENT: No, I thought it.

DONALD: If you thought he wouldn't kill you.

EVANESCENT: First.

DONALD: Do it first.

EVANESCENT: He'd come back. He always does.

DONALD: Do you want me to do it?

EVANESCENT: He'd kill you.

DONALD: You do want me—I'll do it.

EVANESCENT: He'll appear behind your door looking at you looking at yourself in the full-length mirror.

DONALD: He'll fall because the blood will be out of him and he won't be able to get back up.

EVANESCENT: He'll use my blood. It will get him up and through your door.

DONALD: Through my mirror.

EVANESCENT: He follows me to all sides of town. Across the park on his bicycle. I'm running. I think I've lost him. I see him. I tell a policeman, but now he's gone. I go down and across. I'm in yellow. I'm at the apartment. He's up against me, against the mailboxes. Columbus Avenue, the Avenue of the Rapist/Discoverer. He says he'll kill me if I scream. I scream.

DONALD: He kills you.

EVANESCENT: A woman, always out in the hall, is, thank God, again.

DONALD: Still.

EVANESCENT: I'm still. She screams. He turns his knife.

DONALD: Down.

EVANESCENT: I scream it out of his hand. He runs away.

DONALD: With his cock big.

EVANESCENT: Collapsing.

DONALD: Through the mirror.

EVANESCENT: I've been back and back.

DONALD: Four?

EVANESCENT: Five, six times.

DONALD: How'd you get to be his?

EVANESCENT: Would you like to dance?

DONALD: You don't understand the effort. I'm sorry. You do understand.

EVANESCENT: Kill him.

DONALD: Please?

EVANESCENT: You like my hands?

DONALD: Puffy and rough.

EVANESCENT: Just like my feet, but don't tell me.

DONALD: Your lids, nostrils.

EVANESCENT: Lips, nostrils—racial characteristics.

DONALD: I don't mean that.

EVANESCENT: Those.

DONALD: I don't.

EVANESCENT: Those—lips, nostrils.

DONALD: Burns.

EVANESCENT: Kill him.

DONALD: I wouldn't be honest about it.

EVANESCENT: Back him up against those mailboxes and slit his throat.

DONALD: And rape him.

EVANESCENT: I'll do that.

DONALD: Those.

> ALICE *in, but apart from them.*

EVANESCENT: I want to take your course.

DONALD: Teach me to swim.

EVANESCENT: I fall in the water. I lie there. I never get my eyes wet.

> ALICE *speaks.* DONALD, EVANESCENT *do not take HER in.*

ALICE: I'm strong, slow, silent as I do my laps. A few bowls of winesoup before I swim and everything floats by. I tour the great heated pools of Europe ten, twenty, fifty times across. I never count higher. I never count at all. My goal is not numerical, but innumerable intimacies.

DONALD: My eyes go red in the water.

ALICE: I commit myself to chlorine. I want my brown eyes blue.

EVANESCENT: Face down I would die.

ALICE: *Of* the water. Stay of it forever.

EVANESCENT: My mother was in labor with me for sixty hours. I wanted a cigarette every minute.

ALICE: The mist off the water, smoke in my lungs.

EVANESCENT: Wet from dancing.

DONALD: Stinking.

EVANESCENT: I can't keep my dress down. It sticks to my top and slides up my bottom.

ALICE: The rope extends the length of the pool.

EVANESCENT: The rape extends from mailbox to mailbox.

ALICE: A twitch upon the thread and back across I paddle.

DONALD: Bumping through her folds for a slew of grinding kisses I asked my mother if the heyday of her blood were tame.

EVANESCENT: You don't like this music.

DONALD: Swim-Dancer at Two Birds.

ALICE: Honeying and making water over the nasty sty.

ALICE out.

DONALD: There's no place for me in his new society.

EVANESCENT: No place for me.

DONALD: No matter what I've stood for I still wake up in a quiet suburb to the hum of a multitude of birds for whom I don't know the names.

EVANESCENT: I'm called cruel names because I've been with you.

DONALD: But you haven't.

EVANESCENT: Let's give them more to kill me for.

DONALD: No matter where I've gone, chances I've taken, time lost—

EVANESCENT: Time?

DONALD: I still wake up inside this look.

EVANESCENT: You've lost time?

DONALD: What sounds so strange about that?

EVANESCENT: Everything I wear, every car I ride in, everywhere I go is new.

DONALD: Nothing lost. Everything found. As new as you.

EVANESCENT: I refuse to lose a second.

DONALD: On something less than new. Because you in fact are old and won't stop to see it.

EVANESCENT: I refuse.

DONALD: I want everything that I've lost. I want nothing that I have now. I want every detail that displeased me to return. I want to possess the smallest dot and point that annoyed me to exasperation. I will give up everything that I have now, every apparent pleasure, every erotic fulfillment to have again all those things I was convinced were smothering me. I've done nothing but lose time in this massive effort to escape every preposterous jot and tittle I want now engulfing me. I want old and I want it now.

EVANESCENT: My dress sticks to my top and slides up my bottom. I've been here four or five or twelve times. Every time. Every time I say I'm surprised you remember me, but I'm not surprised. If I thought there was a chance you didn't remember me, I'd cut you dead and I be mean when I cut and I do cut dead. Puffy hands cushion the knife. The blade that arches in the night, you motherfucker, and I am the mother you would fuck.

DONALD: I always want it twice when I'm having it once. In the middle of the first, I'm thinking of the second and how badly badassedly I'll have the second. Then the first ends and the second I forget.

EVANESCENT: The second you forget I will cut you.

DONALD: The silk up over your ass, double silk up over your back.

EVANESCENT: Kiss the veins on my eyelids.

DONALD: Grease the wounds 'round your neck.

EVANESCENT: I'm here every time and I'll have you when I want.

DONALD: Tittle I want now engulfing me. I want it old and I want it now.

EVANESCENT: I want you. You are new.

EVANESCENT out. ALICE in.

ALICE: My stories, my stories are more interesting than yours. My stories are definitely more interesting than yours.

DONALD: You could let me finish mine.

ALICE: You never come to the point. You're all trees. This *hemlock*, this *birch*—

DONALD: White and black.

ALICE: This sycamore, this stand of pines, this Dutch Elm disease. There are no images that ever add up to the forest.

DONALD: You have everything reversed. You're the one who gives me every vein in every leaf.

ALICE: Your minutiae suck me dry.

DONALD: You could not be.

ALICE: You give me every red—every—every—grimy green, every grim purple and crimson—

DONALD: You talk colors incessantly. Nothing is mauve enough. Maeve enough.

ALICE: Not a color, not a word.

DONALD: You called my tie—

ALICE: That tie!

DONALD: A sickly grey mauve, a sort of maeve, you said.

ALICE: That tie! Execrable taste you have. Your shoes, those little elf shoes. That tie! We threw that tie straight away— away!

DONALD: You can't redesign me.

ALICE: I must tie you to a suckamore, to a bougainvillea and spread you thin with honey dew—

DONALD: With your two dollar dress, your revolver—

ALICE: With my egg cup I shall go anywhere I please I shall go away from you to anywhere I please.

DONALD out. EARL in.

ALICE: We don't talk about our hopes anymore. Everything has receded.

EARL: From the moment you asked—

ALICE: Don't.

EARL: Are we oversexed? How can we want each other every night if we aren't?

ALICE: You're no longer interested in defying gravity.

EARL: After one of your calling jags, those endless calls you made to protect yourself from knowing I was slipping away—

ALICE: I came to bed immediately after I heard you shower.

EARL: Obviously not immediately or I wouldn't have been there on my side.

ALICE: Asleep.

EARL: Not quite.

ALICE: Quite enough.

EARL: You touched me in that marvelously disinterested way—

ALICE: And gave up.

EARL: Absolute. The giving up.

ALICE: You're fey. Your interests are intense, then they evaporate. I do something unforgivable like leaving the radio on.

EARL: That's a serious matter.

ALICE: Only because you've decided you don't like me anymore.

DONALD in.

DONALD: It is symptomatic. There is a pattern of disinterest—

ALICE: In touching you.

EARL: Disorganization. You're losing grip.

ALICE: And you tell me I am.

DONALD: Of course I do.

    EVANESCENT in.

EVANESCENT: In the interest of truth.

EARL: Yes.

ALICE: You're not interested in truth, only in your interpretation.

DONALD: I deny that.

EVANESCENT: I deny.

EARL: Completely.

ALICE: I get angry.

DONALD: Livid. You make six important phone calls.

EVANESCENT: Very important.

EARL: You announce that this or that person wants us to go here or there and meet so-and-so.

ALICE: Why do you think I'm doing this?

DONALD: I don't know.

EVANESCENT: O, come on.

EARL: You don't want to bury yourself in me, my friends, ideas.

ALICE: Close. As I know I'm losing you, I need to know I have a life apart from you.

DONALD: The life you'll return to—

EVANESCENT: When I allow you to leave. There will be some safety with this or that person going here and there meeting so-and-so.

EARL: I don't want to leave.

ALICE: If you don't want to, we may negotiate.

DONALD *and* EARL: You don't like to think you're the one I'm talking to, but you are.

EVANESCENT *and* ALICE: You'd like to think you're talking to someone else, but you aren't.

EVANESCENT, ALICE.

EVANESCENT: *Vogue.*

ALICE: *The Paris Vogue.*

EVANESCENT: *Cosmo.*

ALICE: So so.

EVANESCENT: *Town and Country.*

ALICE: Ah, *Town and Country.*

EVANESCENT: *The Daily News.*

ALICE: Sometimes good.

EVANESCENT: *Vanity Fair.*

ALICE: Ah, pages in *Vanity Fair. Popular Mechanics* should have one,
the mechanics of the universe. *The New Yorker,* yes, *The New
Yorker* should have one, Talk of the Star Town. *The New
York Times, The Wall Street Journal, The New England Journal of
Medicine, The Economist, The National Review, Psychology Today—*

EVANESCENT: Should get Sydney Omar.

ALICE: *The Sun-Times.*

EVANESCENT: *The Chicago Sun-Times* has the best horoscope in the
world.

ALICE: If not the universe. Except maybe *Town and Country.*

EVANESCENT: Like comparing apples and oranges.

ALICE: Apples and kiwis. I *race* for *Town and Country.*

EVANESCENT: I get *The Sun-Times* express-mailed.

ALICE: "On the 21st, a surprising discovery (as if there's another
kind), will open a new path to money and contracts."
What's today?

EVANESCENT: The 23rd.

ALICE: Impossible.

EVANESCENT: "Be discreet concerning clandestine meeting. You'll make right move at proper moment. Follow through on hunch, instinct."

ALICE: Are you sure?

EVANESCENT: The 23rd.

ALICE: How can that be?

EVANESCENT: You're only two days late.

DONALD, EARL.

DONALD: I don't know why it was called Riverview Park. There was no river within view unless you were at the top of one of the roller coasters and looked south for the fleeting moment at the Chicago River. But then you could see the Polish Roman Catholic Union, but it wasn't called Polish Roman Catholic Union View Park or Stockyards Park or Park Park. The part I remember best was not the Bobs, a ride which threw your stomach up to your throat, or the Chute the Chutes in which you dived headlong into the water with fifty other screamers in a boat or that whirling machine which spun so fast that you were pinned to the sides as the floor came out from under you, but a booth game, a baseball contest of sorts. You'd buy three baseballs for a quarter and then hurl them at a target. The target was in front of a cage in which sat a black man suspended over a vat of brackish water. Hit the nigger, dunk the coon, splash that brack man.

EARL: Mah mamma walk just like she got an oil well in her back yard. Yo mama ain't got no arm, no leg, no smell, no taste, no touch, she ain't nothin' 'less I drill her.

DONALD: It was never obscene.

EARL: What did you say?

DONALD: The target was on the front of the cage, corresponding with the brack man's head or heart or nuts, I do not recall which.

EARL: Your understanding of the situation is that it was never obscene?

DONALD: My Daddy could not walk by those cages, there were three of those brack men—

EARL: Gene, Green and Bean.

DONALD: —without spending a dollar or two.

EARL: Welder, right? Made at that time about $2.14 an hour?

DONALD: Thereabouts.

EARL: He work a whole hour just to rent some baseballs, baseballs just like beer, you done rent 'em, you don't done buy 'em, just to hit mah Daddy in the nuts.

   You pale sack of scumbag shit-for-brains, you throw that ball at me, I come out of this cage and I'll twist your little wienie in wet knots, you gonna pee out yo' ears and shit through your mouth well, shut mah mouf.

We hear a great dunking noise.

DONALD: If the blapperson were really a showman—

EARL: Mah Daddy was, mah Daddy Earl Green of Gene, Green and Bean and the coffee-coated sprouts—mah Daddy was a showman, he was the Show Man.

DONALD: —he would get right back up on his stool and, sopping wet brack man licking drops of brack man's water, taunt that white man.

EARL: How white?

DONALD: So white that he had merged all the colors in his being. He would taunt that man stronger yet.

EARL: Ah'm gonna melt mah fudgesicle in de pinkest folds of yo' mama's dividah, she want me damp 'n brack.

DONALD: Mah Daddy threw and threw—

EARL: Yo' Daddy through and through big bigger bigot got his comeupandoutance when he dropped in his tracks deepest and irretrieveablest dead.

DONALD: Not before he nutsed the socks off Earl Green, a man so brack he was the absence of all color. Mah Daddy so white he was the fulfillment of all pigmentation.

EARL: You say that pig one more time and it will sink into the slime of yo' mama's cuntsciousness.

The dunking noise.

DONALD: Mah Daddy had a very natural aim, he knock down that Miza maybe six, eight times out of twelve.

EARL: Drippingly he get up, his dignity intact. . . .

DONALD, ALICE.

ALICE: When those drunks in the park shouted obscenities—

DONALD: Only one shouted.

ALICE: You weren't there for me. When that one kept coming back and back—

DONALD: After you made eye contact.

ALICE: I had to look at him. It was no mistake.

DONALD: Yes.

ALICE: Cursing violently at me, never at you. At me. My fault for being with you.

DONALD: The pain he felt.

ALICE: The pain! You weren't there for *me*!

DONALD: I took you out of the park.

ALICE: You didn't take me. You never *took* me.

DONALD: Out of the park. I protected you and we didn't hurt him.

ALICE: You knew what had happened to me. You weren't there.

DONALD: I've tried to explain. Then. Now. The man was psychotic—

ALICE: Don't speak to me that way.

DONALD: He was blaming you, but we couldn't blame him back.

ALICE: He was more important to you than I was.

DONALD: He was more hurt than you.

ALICE: You don't see damage when it's in front of you. You knew what had happened to me just before that. The day before, that morning, several things—and yet you let me drown in that too.

DONALD: You didn't drown.

ALICE: I drowned! That drunk shouting—

DONALD: Don't.

ALICE: You heard everything he shouted.

DONALD: I won't let them kill you.

ALICE: Not them. No, not them.

      EARL, DONALD.

EARL: I played four sets of tennis yesterday.

DONALD: Too bad you didn't have an attack.

EARL: At three I did, but the old college try pushed me to four and after that I was fine.

DONALD: So fine, too fine.

EARL: Pardon me, four and a *half* sets.

DONALD: Ten years a set.

EARL: An attack after three.

DONALD: After thirty you had an attack. You won't be twice as old as you are.

EARL: I don't want to be.

DONALD: In not so long you'll get a pet and you'll realize that the pet will outlive you. For the first time. All the other pets you've had until the time you're, say, seventy, will have died before you. But not the one you get then.

EARL: I'm not worrying about leaving a pet alone. Or at least without me. Me buried in my own pet cemetery. That little elephant or donkey will get on quite well without me.

DONALD: Politics never escapes you. Running for office. State Assembly, just for a start?

EARL: Dog catcher. This cat running for dog catcher. Nope, it's Evanescent we want, it's Alice we want on the School Board.

DONALD: Alice is not so sure she wants a child.

EARL: Evanescent wants another.

DONALD: Shit, man—four?

EARL: Don't 'shit, man' me. You and your psuedo-black patois.
    Mah spokesperson, mah spokesong, mah bicycle
    sprocket, rap mah ding-dong docket 'round her
    springsprungsprocket,
your diarrhea of regional racial English.

DONALD: Ah gibs you de straight, clever 'n de cunninglinguish.

EARL: Don't fuck with me, you m-f muthafucker.

DONALD: Re-dun-dundant.

EARL: Ah'm serious, you little peanut dick, now shut the fuck up.

DONALD: What's got into you?

EARL: It's what you're not getting into. Wendy.

DONALD: Wendy who?

EARL: Don't give me your Wendy who shit. You know Wendy who, shit.

DONALD: Spare me your—
    Hey, that was nice. Do that again. Don't give me your Wendy who shit. Is that it? I got it now. Don't give me your Wendy who shit. You know Wendy who shit. Man, that's writing. I love it. Good writing likes to be written well, yohsuh.

EARL: You call her again—

ALICE in.

ALICE: Call her again what?

EVANESCENT.

EVANESCENT: It was a little string tie that was, oh, 24 inches long with a big longhorn holding the ends together. You've seen them, you can expand them far enough so you don't have to untie them altogether, just loosen them up enough to slip around your neck and then you kind of tighten the longhorn up close to the neck. Bet you've seen it on all kinds of men. Used to be a little more popular than they are now. Or maybe they're coming back some, I don't rightly know. That was his main tie. He had another tie, clip-on kind he didn't have to tie at all, knot always perfect, so he said, looked to me always a bit 'burcular— 'burcular—tube-burcular, don't know quite what I mean, like a tube, like a pus-cock about to burst, peacock heart about to burst—

> Sometimes I feel like a motherfuckerless child
> Sometimes I feel like a motherfuckerless child
> Sometimes I feel

ALICE.

ALICE: My Daddy used to lift me very high on his shoulder/look myself in the mirror/very tall on the wall/mirror mirror o so tall and I wasn't wearing nothing at all/nothing/ and I used to sit with my little self against the back of his neck and he used to put on a heavy shirt starched heavy starched and lift me up around so my little self could settle up against his collar my little self gettin' slightly abrased bish bash bash my little self and he'd get his tie out slide it 'round underneath his collar my little self bein' slid around 'round the back of his collar, then slidin' one end over the other and through/Windsor knot, baby?, he'd ask/Windsor knot, Daddy, I'd say/Windsor Windsor on the wall/ Daddy 'frow up on us all.

EARL.

EARL: Sinbad the Gorilla was the featured ape at the Lincoln Park
Zoo from 1940 to 1950 something. Every weekend di-
vorced fathers from Kalamazoo to Kankakee brought
their little bairns past the bears and cubbies of Chicago to
the mainest attraction, the baddest, posilutely the worst
two to four-legged creeachur in capital big tent captivity.
The elephants of all sexes, the lions, the tigers were just
little pussycats. The Missa, the Mister and the Massa's
Mastodon held no trunk and truck next to Sinbad the
Boyilla of all Girlillas.

Sinbad just sitting on his scale watching his avoirdupois
tipping over into the recesses of the uprights' walking and
talking. "Lookee here," say my Daddy, "how Sinnerbad-
dest lean out from his tiny stool and taunt us grand and
baby and uprights, the pianos of humanity, to play a song
he can't crush with his bee-bop rendition of 23 Men on a
Dead Ape's Chest."

Meantime there is this old white lady who's yelling for
some zookeeper to stop Sin from playing with himself
which he's not doing seriously, but only lazy-like, kind of
funnin', lil' jolt now and then, kind you get in the shower
now and then. I think my Daddy does not know if she's
complaining about him, being pretty juiced by now with
the beer and the Smirnoff he's been guzzling, but he pays
her no mind and instead puts all his considerable power
toward mucking 'round with Sinbad. My Daddy picks up
this baseball, three for a quarter and says, "Ah'm heavin'
this beanball at the mark right above Sinbad's head or
heart or nuts and when this ball hits that mark that m-f
Sinbad gonna' fall off his stool-scale with all his avoirdupois and take a dunk in that tank of slime-water 'cause
Ah'm the teacher of record and that ape's goin' to school."

Mah Daddy took this ball he carried with him at all
times and, thinking we were in the Riverview Amusement
Park with the three colored mens in the ribber rubber
suits just yellin' at the white folk, darin' 'em to 'frow up
fast balls, Daddy, pretty juiced, heaves up this 'frowup,
but it hits the bars keepin' us from Sinbad and ricochets

onto old white lady and she screams and Sinbad gets his
ass up and sticks his dick out at old white lady and pisses
her all 'cross the eyeballs and Daddy and SinSin the Baddest slap hands give each other the low fives, fart like two
horses in a crowd and me and Daddy run down the lane
pretending we free.

I looked back and I saw Sinbad laughing, crying and into
some deadly serious pulling of that master pud.

EARL *in silhouette,* DONALD.

DONALD: We shall arrest you, detain you, not charge you. We
shall reason with you, we shall encourage you to see our
truth and then we shall beat you. Upside the head. We
shall damage your spine. Irreparably. We shall challenge
your spirit. You shall be allowed to resist this challenge to
your spirit. Indeed, you shall be allowed to resist to the
limits of your ability. If you wish. This is completely up to
you. At an appropriate time we shall transport you 800 to
1000 miles, depending upon our choice of destination, in
the back of a vehicle especially chosen for such purposes.
During the journey we shall provide you with every op-
portunity to defecate standing up. We know what it is to
have to hold it, as it were. We shall also allow you not to
wear any clothing so as not to prevent your body from
experiencing both the heat and the cold of the day and the
night. You shall have with you as your companions six
soldiers armed to the teeth, lest you feel any lack of
security on this, your maiden voyage across the veld.
These men and one woman shall show you every sexual
courtesy, that is, curtsey, that is they shall show you how
to curtsey, which you shall then do while their rifle-butts
bum-fuck you into erotic frenzy. Upon arrival, after eigh-
teen hours of expert driving, you shall be shown your cell.
If your accommodations are unsatisfactory, do not despair, for what's left of your spirit shall not remain there
long. We shall allow you to hang yourself in your cell with
a tie we'll provide you, your personal tie. This tie shall not
hang anyone else. You have our word. Amplification: it is
your personal tie, but it is our club tie, purple and crimson,

a straight tie not too narrow, not too wide, a regimental
sort of tie, which we shall give you, the tie that binds you
to the community of our brotherhood, Der Broederbond.
You shall indeed be bloody, but you shall remain un-
bowed, indeed, unbow-tied.
   Praise be the Lord for the Mighty have fallen.

EVANESCENT.

EVANESCENT: In Frenchy Griffin's Tonsorial Palace of Art, first
   time I be straightening out some foul follicle behavior, all
   the men smoking those Gauloises stolen right off a Mont-
   real ship docked in Lake Wishagain. Frenchy said, never
   get no cough, this tobacco pure, pure rolled-up straw and
   cowcake. I read the National Police Gazette upon the
   death of Dorothy Dandridge, you know how she died?,
   the strangest way, she swallowed a little pin, pin-prick,
   no, it was a needle got in her ankle somehow, no, it was a
   sliver from some gin mill on the Mahogany Trail, she slid
   her many cheeks along, no, it was pin, pin-prick, needle,
   sliver, silver bullet of a needle somehow getting up under
   her skin and travelling all the way 'round and 'round and
   stabbing her right through her sacred scared heart. Dorothy, you be my Dorothy, the Wizardress of Oz and I
   wanted so much to be like you, shimmering, silvering in
   the black-white light of your oh-so-glamorous silkily re-
   laxed hair. Relax, hair, relax and shake me into the futu-
   ristics of needles and pin-pricks.

EARL.

EARL: We go down to the swamp to get initiated in the rights of
   the heavy hoodooboodoo. With the eye of bat and the
   esophagoose of newt we gulpin' down the pancreatic
   noose of sweetbreads round my arterial highways
   through the inner city of my aorta/lizard gizzards/another
   yet another orta of fried pork rinds making stone of rinds
   rhinestoned through my prostrate prostate state of pros-
   thesis/it be my thesis that the black cookery bookery is
   guaranteed with the bite of phlebitis and the gouge of

gout/lay up every black man and boy so the quadzillion double bypass do him no good/no little bugger going to pass through our endzone no witch way the way of the witch and her incantations/abracazebra we be white in the flour we roll in/keep us sliding next to the carp so slick and grease-poppingly smooth/splat in the one eye/we still see some shapes/serve 'em up say 'em up with some mumbo-gumbo some corn sicklikker and the wonder of it all is that the black man is alive at all. And that is the credit that we are to this race and you may say it with me—that the black man is alive at all—that given what we have been consuming over the centuries since we have been in the Americas pouring down the fiery bile on outstretched paper thin bladders who have the gall and the gall and the gall, that given what we have been dumping on our 26 feet of intestine—dear Lord, why couldn't you give us 52, that given all those givens, that we have embraced every conceivable way and Pall Mall and Kool to bootblack our lungs, that given the most magniferous givens, it is a wondiferous wonderment most fantastigorical that the black man has not extincted himself from God's green Amen Corner with yet another bucket of double-crisp chittlins. Praise the Lord and pass the ammu-fishfry!

DONALD.

DONALD: The folks next door were Russians, the Romashkos. John Romashko, the father. Not a drinker, not a Smashko. A philanderer, possibly, but not the problem. A used-car salesman—the problem. John'd stay away three four days at a time, not a sales binge, just keeping away from the Law, sitting out in front of the house. He'd come home when the coast was clear and he and his wife May would fight all night. Furious screaming, no smashing, no smashing of plates, but yelling all in Russian before air conditioning, summer heat'd like to fry your eyeballs, windows open, seventeen mosquitoes skating over your blood, you wanted to reach out through your window, across the gangway and touch Tanya's window, Tanya, daughter of John and May, and say, I'm sorry, Tanya, your old man's a

crook, but just think he doesn't smoke rolled-up Camel
shit, does not throw baseballs at red-eyed black guys, does
not provide the means and the ways by which you swallow cold cash and every morning after every fight night,
John in his three-piece suit and two-toned shoes and his
hand-painted tie brown and orange and yellow and red,
yes sir, red and orange and yellow and brown getting
down coming down his stairs, John all stroked and
slacked-back, razor-creased and perfect-cuffed, slick-
headed dude, brilliantined and brilliant-tied.

Hi there John, hi there young man, what a deep deep
pleasure it is to be alive and please take care of my little
Tanya. I wanted to say, John, I will slide down her sun-
strap and take sucksuch good care of that shoulder, especially that day when news came back that John had died
the deepest death at the wheel of a '47 DeSoto stick shift
at the shoulder slump slump at the side of Tanya's sun-
strap my Daddy always looked that Tanya up and down.

Do not grieve, John, we shall take good care and we did
buy your hand-painted tie.

ALICE.

ALICE: After the operation—it's a quick suck and scrape job, you
know what it is—I want to the Hyatt House to have a
drink, 11:30, noon, thereabouts and I amazingly didn't
want one, so I went to wash my euphemism, nearly
tripped on the wet marble, gave the lady a dollar or five,
Lincoln, five, and went into the hallway, sat between the
lavatories and watched the women go by, ranking, rating
their legs, hair, dress, ankles, shoes and a cowgirl, buxom,
bleached, burned-out, tassels, fringes, buckboard grease
all about her pouches, chaps down the sides but not the
fronts of her fat thighs all prominent and pushing ahead,
making her spurs jingle jangle jingle and about the fourth
time she walked up and down she looked at me the first
time and she sat next to me and said, "Darlin', I've had
children by four different men and I've never been married" and I said, "I been married four times and I ain't had
no child yet."

Thanks, Daddy, for this latest money from afar for my operation so aclose and if you're ever down and out and they send you to the V.A. hospital, I sure will send you a pair of socks.

EVANESCENT.

EVANESCENT: After the photos came out, I was standing on 56th and 8th Avenue, waiting for something to happen besides disaster when a very, I have to say it, butchie white woman came walking slowly by with magazine in hand, I mean in face, a wonder she didn't fall right through the fish store window, couldn't believe Miss America would be diddling no woman, white, black or blue for anybody with $4 to stare—spare—she stopped dead, jaw aslack and looked up at me, you seen one kind of Miss America you see 'em all and she did this double-take when she knew I was staring at her staring at *her* off the glossies and she did this about-face and went back the other way, slapped that maggie front and back together leaving me to wonder what my Daddy would have said before the cameras about his daughter before the camera, dirty-eye prick that it is.

DONALD.

DONALD:
You jutht gibth me yo' whyfe fo' lil re-hear-thal
we gonna' re-hear 'n re-thee-thal thome incuntationth boil up
    de cauldron fo' de canniballjithmth
we taketh de ringth frub our notheth 'n burnth them into de
    flesh 'roun'de nippleth den we cutth them off den eatth
    'em thizzlin
jutht lil re-hear-thal 'n re-eat-thal
jutht gib me yo whyfe
jutht gib me, pretty pleath fo' her nippleth

EARL.

EARL: I wanted to be an actor so badly. I worked very hard at every phase of preparation and I had confidence that I at least had a shot. Our Father—that extraordinary Jesuit,

Father Walsh—he was Father, nothing more, Father put
me in some plays and I think I was o.k. but scared, scared. I
played the poet Cinna in a modern dress version of Julius
Caesar. Lots of black leather jackets, tights. Cinna gets
killed because the rabble thinks he's another Cinna, so the
poet gets to die, me, I get to. After opening, Father asked
to see me. Like an audience with the Pope. At least. We
went into this little office and he had me sit next to him so
we were facing the same direction and he said, "Earl, you'll
never be an actor unless until you lose your black speech."
I'm not saying that's why I've made the odd blaxploitation
film.

ALICE: Odd or infrequent?

DONALD: Not so infrequent

EVANESCENT: *Catfish Fry, Super Catfish Fry, Son of Super Catfish Fry.*

EARL: There were some good things in those films.

ALICE does the Joan Rivers vomit.

EARL (*to ALICE*): So you do yet another test script for *Search for
Loving* or the *Guiding Tomorrow*. You think that's an accomp-
lishment?

DONALD: The little Miss Jackie Robinson of daytime television.

ALICE (*to DONALD*): You think having the account for Kraft salad
dressing is advancing the cause of humanity.

EVANESCENT: Please please cool it, we have our party to experience.

ALICE: What happened to you guys and your runs for political
office?

EVANESCENT: Change your party career.

ALICE: You're 45 years old. Go into Public Health. Get your
Master's of Bad Ass, M.B.A., your M.fucking F.fucking A.,
your Masters of Shit Work from the School of Columbian
welfare, your J.D., Juris Dickoff, but do something and
make your mark.

EVANESCENT: Or go hang.

The Four in tableaux. FATHER comes in.

FATHER: I came out of Nebraska in 1930 and headed for Chicago
with my valise, my $2 revolver and my suit and tie. Wide
open town let you live easy on coffee and Camels slinging
beef and pork at the Wimpies on Wabash, $5 a week, $4,
whatever came in cain't make it in Chicago, cain't make it,
what was said. Took some time off, on the bum, rode the
rails back out West, cross Canada, down through Idaho
with a buddy, stopped to pick potatoes, 1931–32, me a slim
fellow, long arms, bending over picking, picking after two
days like to die, my buddy, fat man, not sore yet, making
fun of me, 4 days go by, I've worked into it and fat man
now suffering, he did die on the train back to Chicago,
back at Wimpies, Pronto-Pup, that was a place, batter-
wrapped dogs deep-fried, take up residence right below
your heart, cain't make it in Chicago, service, Navy, 1934–
38, China Sea, Philippines, radio man, Chicago, welding
school, 4 a.m., bus, train, subway, East Chicago, Indiana,
Chicago, Victoria, marry Victoria, factory, noise, hearing
loss, polisher, m'man the polisher, steam-fitter, my other
man, song-dance team, weekends, Gene, Green 'n Bean,
South Side, children, punch bag, basement, Camels, bathroom, Stockyards, shirt pockets, Camel-filled, nose jam
shittn' smoke, sugar Daddy, smear poo 'frow up 'frow up,
attack, clutch chest, 'sposin' myself, outhibited, Sinbad the
Sailor, Riverview Park. Ah'm gonna melt mah fudgesicle
in de pinkest folds of yo' mama's dividah, she want me
damp 'n brack Windsor Windsor on the wall

A man fathers children. One has abortions, one poses
lewdly for photographs, one shoots films which exploit
everyone including oneself, one writes speeches, copy,
without spiritual substance, one works for a soap opera,
one goes to parties, one sneaks from room to room, one
prowls the parks, one pins others against mailboxes, one
brutalizes all others, each one would string up all others,
each one would hang all others until their tongues
reached down so far they licked the very genitalia they
have subjected others to. In this most possible of all possible worlds, where the greatest good is the greatest
number, where sex is maisured against two orangutans
having a bad insulin reaction, at the very least, Lord, do
Lord, wormwood, give me my voice and give me light.

HE leaves. The Four out of tableaux.

EARL: I'm not saying that—

EVANESCENT: I'm not saying that—

DONALD: I'm not saying that—

ALICE: I'm not saying that—

AL FOUR: I'm not saying that—

ALICE: Nice Congregationalist woman come into the p.o. the other day with a great big old dog, Arthur she calls him, arthritic, the oldest, saddest, used-to-be-meanest dog, the smellinest, fartinest, moldiest, scraggliest mustard gas spewingest out its front and back dog like one of those Russian Baryshnikov dancing rifles.

EARL: Kalishnikov.

ALICE: Automatic ratatatshat and she says, "It's the Koreans, you know what those Koreans do?"

EARL: They hang their dogs.

ALICE: "They hang their dogs."

EARL: And they call themselves civilized.

DONALD starts to sing "Sittin' in la la, Waitin' for my ya ya." EVANESCENT starts to dance. Both continue until end of play. DONALD does not dance.

ALICE: "They find the sweetest little puppy and they raise that puppy with the children, with the family and they love that little puppy to pieces and when that puppy is one year old they all go out on a picnic and they're preparing the charcoal and the spit and the puppy's runnin' 'round so happy and care-free and then the Father takes this lovely little creature and he ties him 'round the neck and he ties that tie to a tree limb and he lets that puppy hang and the puppy thinks it's just a little game and the Father goes back and he lights the coals and the puppy twists and twists and the puppy dies and these Koreans they eat the little puppy roasted and the little children get the first bites."